DECIPHERING
THE GOLDEN FLOWER
ONE SECRET AT A TIME

JJ Semple

A Life Force Books Publication

Disclaimer: The information in this book is for educational purposes only, and is not intended as medical advice. Neither the author nor the publisher of this work will be held accountable for any use or misuse of the information contained in this book. Because there is always some risk involved, the author, the publisher, and/or the distributors of this book are not responsible for any effects or consequences from the use of any suggestions, recommendations, or procedures described hereafter.

Author's Note: Due to the privacy concerns of individuals portrayed in this book, some of the events were expanded or changed. Some of the individuals portrayed are composites of more than one person and many names and identifying characteristics have been changed.

The author made all reasonable efforts to contact all literature sources quoted in the text.

Life Force Books
PO Box 302
Bayside, CA 95524
www.lifeforcebooks.com

ISBN: 978-0-9795331-1-2

Printed in the United States of America

DECIPHERING
THE GOLDEN FLOWER
One Secret At a Time

The greatest book in the world, the Mahabharata, tells us we all have to live and die by our karmic cycle. Thus works the perfect reward-and-punishment, cause-and-effect, code of the universe. We live out in our present life what we wrote out in our last. But the great moral thriller also orders us to rage against karma and its despotic dictates. It teaches us to subvert it. To change it. It tells us we also write out our next lives as we live out our present.

- *The Alchemy of Desire*—Tarun J. Tejpal

Table of Contents

To women in general, to Madeleine,
Margo, Martine, Gloria,
and Donna especially.

Self-realization begins at birth; it is the journey as much as it is the destination.

~ Araminta Matthews

Introduction

This book is a remarkable autobiography starting with the "splinter accident" in the author's childhood. Harmless at first glance, the incident turns into a traumatic, haunting experience resulting in a chain reaction of failures in the author's early life.

After several decades of failure, through the accidental discovery of secret meditation techniques, the author awakens the power of Kundalini (evolutionary Life Force energy) and learns the breadth of his deficiencies. As a result, he struggles to regain his spiritual and physical equilibrium, what the author calls "symmetry."

The reader is impressed by the author's profound self-study, his willingness to admit failure, his sensitivity and awareness in grasping and deciphering his true nature—often with the help of strong females who act like beacons of sanity in his erratic early life.

Furthermore, with its captivating narrative power, the book succeeds in transferring his first hand experiences and feelings to the reader.

In his final message, JJ Semple focuses on how to activate the hidden potential of our unique beings, which is actually laid out for each of us in a "blueprint" before our birth. Thus, the book stirs us to self-reflection, reminds us to concentrate on true pertinent values, all the while encouraging and showing us how to avoid addiction while leading a more natural life.

Helmut A. Schaeffer, Ph.D
Berlin, 14 August, 2006

Prologue

I did not know then what I came to grasp later on—that an automatic mechanism, forced by the practice of meditation, had suddenly started to function with the object of reshaping my mind to make it fit for the expression of a more heightened and extended consciousness, by means of biological processes as natural and as governed by inviolable laws as the evolution of the species or the development and birth of a child.[1]

> - *Kundalini: The Evolutionary Energy in Man*—Gopi Krishna

There's an accident. A seven-year-old boy is rushed to the hospital. His parents spare no expense: the best care, the finest doctors, and soon life is back to normal. Months later, however, when he returns to school, there are ominous signs, such as the sudden erosion of his cognitive abilities. Can there be a link to the accident? No one, including his parents, believes so. Yet the signs are unmistakable. At first he just feels different. Gradually, however, he watches his body change—his looks, his abilities, his personality, every part of him—until as a teenager, he realizes he's no longer the same person. Only after years of failure does he discover a secret resource within his body that enables him to understand how the accident affected him.

I am that boy, and I still have trouble believing there was a link between that accident and my subsequent implosion. But a link there was. My conscious mind tried to suppress it. Yet, as I grew older, more concerned about my health and the direction of my life, I started to investigate. I read many books, tried many remedies, and talked to many wise people. All to no avail. It took me more than thirty years of Yogic practice to discover the hidden capabilities of my body.

The early part of my life is a catalogue of failures. None of these anecdotes is meant to shock, discourage or offend. Like parables, they illustrate how dysfunctional behavior takes root when the body's natural symmetry is disrupted. At first, my future seemed bleak—like so many others searching for redemption. Malcolm X was a pimp; Saint Peter renounced Jesus; Milarepa was a murderer. Did those acts disqualify them from redemption? On the contrary, their most shameful acts were turning points.

By telling my story the way I lived it, with all the warts and blemishes apparent, you will understand how, amidst all the uncertainties of life, against all odds, I was swept out of a desperate situation and handed the means of attaining self-knowledge. For my story is your story. You possess this power.

My story begins at birth, or, more accurately, just before conception. We are all perfect at that split-second moment before conception. Of course, like a building before the foundation is laid, at that moment our beings are only blueprints. These blueprints—the numinous plans laid out for our substantiation—are perfect. At the moment of conception—the moment the egg is fertilized by the sperm—the body begins to take shape. It's the moment when, were we able to stand over our perfect blueprints, we might wonder if they can be executed as designed. That's the job of the Life Force. The Life Force has many names: Kundalini[2], sublimation, Tantra, alchemy, serpent power, primordial energy, cosmic power, Qi, Reiki, and Primal Spirit. Until the moment of birth, the Life Force controls our substantiation. The moment we are born we become conscious and our natural life force becomes inactive. After we're born, something always seems to interfere with our continued growth. We get sick, accidents occur, we become addicted, we grow older, our bodies break down. It's not that things can't happen while we are in the womb, they can. By and large, however, our time in the womb is peaceful. But after we are born, the frequency of interference increases because that's when we start doing things to ourselves. That's when we bring our will, or lack of it, to bear. That's when the serious damage is done.

Most of the time we just go on living. What else is there to do? That's the irony of the Life Force: just when we need it most, it becomes dormant. *If only the blueprint could have been realized without interference*—the operative expression being *realized without interference*. By that I mean without some stimulus altering the growth process.

There are two types of stimuli: those under our control and those beyond our control. For example, most birth defects are beyond our control. They occur in many ways, from genetic imperfections to externally induced toxic chemicals to harmful vaccinations to illness or addiction in the expectant mother's body. The pathology of stimuli outside our control is beyond the scope of this book. Not being a pathologist, I don't know much about them. I do, however, know about the stimuli under my control. I've explored them at length during the struggle to return my body to its original symmetrical state.

The stimuli under our control are the substances we ingest, the ideas we adhere to, the influences, forces and conditions we subject ourselves to, the addictions we form, the choices we make. From the moment we're born, any one of thousands of stimuli—within or out of our control—can alter our growth, assuring degrees of deviation from the blueprint for our unique bodily substantiation.

If it's under our control, we are responsible. In any case, responsible or not, because of the nature of life—its accidents and its addictions—we are at risk of deviating from the plan for our perfect body. It happened to me.

Yet while it was happening, I never stopped yearning for the perfection I'd lost. Why? Because intuitively I sensed I was becoming someone else, someone other than whom I was meant to be. Of course, I didn't realize I was growing away from my perfect body. In fact, I didn't know I possessed a perfect body—one designed for me before my birth. Now that doesn't mean I had short toes and two heads, it simply means I was not the individual I was meant to be. The degree of deformity is determined by the toxicity of the stimulus.

I know it's hard to believe. You may say: *Who cares? I'm fine the way I am.* As with everything, the degree of caring is relative. But suppose you realized you *were* growing away from your perfect body. How much would it bother you and how much effort would you expend to remedy the situation?

I submit that if it bothers you and you want to remedy the situation, then you are already on the path to restoration, the path of self-knowledge. There's one thing about self-knowledge. Once you're attracted to it, you'll be driven to delve deeper. And you will find it. Not just in dribs and drabs, but in the form of a science, an empirical science based on the study of the human body, your body. It took me years to discover that a science of empirical self-knowledge actually existed. I now realize that I was looking for empirical self-knowledge all my life, even in my most self-destructive moments. Once I got a taste of it, I wanted to learn more. I acted compulsively, determined to go to any lengths to repair the damage to my being, the damage done by my accident. Luckily, my discoveries led me to a means of activating the Life Force, the only way of correcting the damage done by my accident.

• • •

This book is also about healing. It begins with the injury that rendered my perfect body imperfect. There's a lot to be learned from imperfection. Believing you're perfect, you see yourself as *The Standard*. Imperfect, you are intuitively drawn to perfection and search for it everywhere.

In 1972, when I was thirty-four, a stranger handed me a book called *The Secret of the Golden Flower*. It was a serendipitous moment, my introduction to empirical science and the beginning of my healing process. I didn't realize it at the time. In fact, I put the book away for over a year. Sometime later however, I picked it up and began practicing the method of meditation in the text. At first I thought I was wasting my time.

Three months into my practice, however, my body started changing. Profound psychological and mental changes occurred as well, but the bulk of the transformations occurred in my physical body. Moreover, once the transformations began, my body took over on its own. How can the body take over and effectively transform itself? Very simply, I had aroused a power within myself known as Kundalini. Friends to whom I described my experience—the ones who had the patience to listen—humored me. They granted me some sort of spiritual epiphany, but cautioned that it had really only happened in my mind. I told them no, my body was being torn apart and rebuilt. I told them Kundalini was potent enough to accomplish this metamorphosis, like the crab that sheds his shell and grows a new one. What do you suppose their reaction was?

You'll find out in the chapters ahead. But first I want to describe some of the far-reaching implications of my experience—just to give you an idea of the power of perfection, because Kundalini is perfection. That doesn't mean a person who awakens it is perfect. Far from it; he or she is still a fallible man or a woman. But should a person submit to Kundalini, over time its power is capable of restoring that individual to a pristine, perfect state.

It happened to me. After activating the Kundalini-Life Force, I was able to see the blueprint of my perfect body and compare it to my altered state. Amazingly, the Life Force recognized my deformity and immediately began to correct it. I witnessed it slowly reshape my body to the exact proportions in the blueprint.

Deciphering the Golden Flower

So how does Kundalini heal the body? By using the body's own communication network—the nervous system. For example, suppose you saw halfway through a tree branch. The branch continues to live, but compared to its undamaged counterparts, the sawed branch begins to wither. Leaves fall off, twigs and branches turn brittle, and eventually the limb dies. Trees, you see, have no means of revitalizing damaged limbs. They don't bother with them; they merely grow new ones. Unlike trees that simply grow new branches, we humans have no limbs to spare. We do, however, possess a mechanism for regeneration—Kundalini.

I was like a tree with withering limbs. Fortunately, I learned how to revitalize myself. It's a method I call Golden Flower Meditation (GFM), a system I developed after numerous readings of and experimentation with *The Secret of the Golden Flower*, a book I call *The Empirical Science Bible*. Practicing GFM resulted in the awakening of my Kundalini-Life Force.

Now I'm not the only one interested in neural revitalization. Doctors and researchers are, too. That's right, my empirical research, performed on myself over the last thirty years, has led me to a crossroads with traditional medicine. With one difference: I take an inside-out approach while traditional medicine takes an outside-in approach.

Before I go into the differences, I want to tell you what researchers have accomplished. It will help you compare the two approaches. The research I refer to began with the problem of chronic pain. Do you know what doctors call chronic pain? RSD, or reflex sympathetic dystrophy. And it dates back awhile.

In the October 10, 2005 *New Yorker* article by Jerome Groopman: "During the Civil War, Dr. S. Weir Mitchell served as a surgeon for the Union Army and treated soldiers wounded by bayonets, sabers and bullets. Some continued to complain of severe pain long after the injuries—typically an arm or a leg—had healed, and Mitchell noticed that these men had other symptoms in common: burning pain, accompanied by swelling, redness, and temperature fluctuations in the injured limb."[3]

The same *New Yorker* article fast-forwards to 1946, "Other physicians adopted the term *causalgia* to refer to a pain syndrome that occasionally developed in a limb after an injury or a medical procedure."[4] Still later in the article, Harvard Medical School Assistant Professor, Anne Louise Oaklander explains, "Patients with RSD were often dismissed as being neurotic, self-serving, or somatizing. Then you meet them. You realize that they are reasonable people, and you see them in clinic periodically and it becomes clear that this is not a psychiatric disorder." The article concludes, "When one of her RSD patients fails to improve with medication, Oaklander considers a surgical option which entails implanting an electrical stimulator in the limb or near the spine to send benign impulses at regular intervals along the injured nerve. Once the stimulator is implanted, the patient can turn it on or off by holding a special magnet over the skin, and some eventually find they no longer need to turn it on. Thousands of people have received stimulators, though complications, such as infection and electrode malfunction, are common."[5]

And that's the difference between outside-in and inside-out. A foreign object implanted under the skin, the electrical stimulator works from the outside-in. Using the body's own hidden resources, GFM works from the inside-out. It activates the healing power of the Life Force, which, in turn, repairs the damaged members by sending vital energy throughout the nervous system. Through meditation the nervous system is stimulated such that the natural chemical substances of body are recombined and used for healing.

So—and this requires a leap of logic—if I could see the original design for my body and it was perfect in every way, there must be some sentient agency that created this design. And even though my growth took a detour on account of my deformity, the blueprint continued to exist in some ethereal computer-memory-like storage, waiting for the day that I might learn of its existence and find a way back to it.

Happily, GFM, the method of meditation I practiced, restored my deformed body to its original state, and, in so doing, proved both the existence of the blueprint and the restorative power of the Kundalini-Life Force. This sounds an awful lot like Intelligent Design, doesn't it? A permanent blueprint of our beings and a mechanism within the body capable of restoring it to its intended state. It sounds like it, but is it?

First of all, I feel uncomfortable even discussing Intelligent Design (ID), especially against today's backdrop of socio-political controversy. As soon as one utters the words Intelligent Design, people roll their eyes. It's a concept that needs an overhaul. Trouble is, it's already had an overhaul. Its antecedent, so-called Creation Science, was even more controversial and a lot less credible, especially in scientific circles. For the sake of argument, however, let's take a dispassionate look at ID. The problem is not really that ID is inherently ludicrous or silly; it's merely that instead of trying to prove it, its proponents have attacked the basis of the scientific method, thereby alienating the entire scientific community. Instead of looking for evidence to prove their theory—and that's all Intelligent Design is, a theory—they attacked evolution, saying that life is too complicated to be explained by science. But because they could offer no proof of their own theory, ID remains just that—a theory. So why does this particular theory provoke such an uproar? Well, it's really social politics, isn't it? The ID proponents who attempted to force schools to replace the teaching of evolution with Intelligent Design were perceived to be playing politics.

If it weren't for this political maneuvering, ID as a theory should pose no threat to anyone. Its proponents, if they wanted to prove their theory, would spend their time searching for empirical proofs, not trying to discredit or impugn other fields. After all, Gopi Krishna himself declared, "There would be no intelligence in us if there were no intelligence in the universe."6 The difference between Gopi Krishna and today's proponents of ID is the former investigated ID empirically.

Following his lead, I uncovered additional empirical evidence of Intelligent Design. My inquiry, however, does not constitute a repudiation of evolution. In fact, the two are not mutually exclusive. I didn't use either "scientific rationalism" or "divine inspiration" to investigate Intelligent Design; I used GFM and personal observation, techniques of the empirical Life Force scientist.

Don't take my word for anything I say; I don't want you to. I want you to find out for yourself. For Kundalini is not something that can be observed in a Petri dish or isolated by medical experiments or psychological testing. The power I discovered is systemic.

It works with the rest of the body functioning around it. And if it worked for me, it will work for you. That is, if you approach it correctly. What is the correct approach? This book explains my approach in detail. I don't leave anything out. By the end of the book you'll have learned from my mistakes. In fact, you'll be an expert.

So does my experience validate Intelligent Design? A suitable metaphor might be a computer game a child plays for many years. Over time he masters the game, until it becomes boring. One day, an older, more experienced friend tells him about a secret code that opens up new levels of complexity. When he uses the secret code, the new features challenge him and the game becomes full of wonder again. Does he reflect on the designer who foresaw his gradual loss of interest? Or does he accept his good fortune and move ahead?

I have accepted my good fortune and moved on, secure in the knowledge that science and ID are not mutually exclusive. My experience with *The Secret of the Golden Flower* showed me that there is a dormant Life Force in our beings. This metaphysical entity—the *Primal Spirit* as it's called in *The Secret of the Golden Flower*—is a reflection in us of Nature's undivided entirety.

It is as real as the physical sub-systems of our body: the digestive system, the nervous, the respiratory, the cardiovascular systems. Although it exists side-by-side with the body's major physical systems, it can only be activated through the techniques of highly refined meditation methods like GFM.

I realize a postulate like this attracts skepticism, and that's normal, especially since its actuality lies beyond the material world. That's why I use the term metaphysical, because it lies beyond the physical; it cannot be seen or touched.

When we dig deeper, however, we discover that life is loaded with unresolved mysteries. For instance, we were not able to *see* the endocrine or lymphatic systems with the tools of early medicine. We had to wait for more advanced technology. So it's important not to put limits on science because what we designate today as reality will be different tomorrow. Why be so eager to say: show this *Primal Spirit* to me now, or admit it doesn't exist?

Unfortunately, we can't go out and purchase a gadget for awakening the *Primal Spirit*. To apprehend it, we must master the secret meditation techniques revealed in this book. Once activated, however, the Life Force heals the physical systems of the body. In fact, there's a little understood cause and effect relationship between the physical and metaphysical. Physical actions, such as diaphragmatic deep breathing, control of heart rate, and the other secret techniques mentioned throughout this book activate the metaphysical entity, which, in turn, restores the physical systems to their optimal states.

Activating the metaphysical entity (*Primal Spirit* and *Life Force* are other names for this entity) pays dividends in the form of bodily rejuvenation. Instead of slowly dissipating our energies over a lifetime as individuals who ignore the *Primal Spirit* do, those who activate the *Primal Spirit* spark a rebirth, a release of pure Life Force energy throughout their beings.

Whether you believe me or not cannot be resolved by debate. Debate puts dabblers on the same footing with adepts, like Talk Radio—a modern Tower of Babel, a cacophony of ignorant and intelligent voices that ultimately drag the intelligent voices down to the level of ignorance.

The fact that I can see my original design and it is perfect means to me that an unseen sentient entity in nature created it before my being came into this world. As someone who has reactivated this Life Force entity and watched it rejuvenate my body's physical systems and restore my symmetry, worshiping it is the furthest thing from my mind. I want to understand it, to make it available to others.

My guiding purpose, therefore, like that of the child with his newly enhanced game, is to revel in my discovery and let its wondrous power continue to help me evolve. At the same time, I feel bound to tell my story to those interested in empirical knowledge, particularly, those readers looking for information on activating the Life Force in order to take advantage of its extraordinary restorative healing powers.

1—Accident

...That these men,
Carrying, I say, the stamp of one defect,
Being nature's livery or fortune's star,
His virtues else, be they pure as grace,
As infinite as man may undergo,
Shall in the general censure take corruption
From that particular fault.

- *Hamlet*—William Shakespeare

I have a first memory, one of the few before my accident. I run into our Manhattan townhouse, right through my mother's cocktail party. I'm upstairs before she can ask me about the birthday party I've been to. I shut the bathroom door, take off my Eton[7] jacket, stuff it in the toilet and start to flush.

When my mother connects my absence to what she later calls "a plumbing noise," she quietly excuses herself from the party and follows me upstairs.

"I found you in the bathroom. You were shoving your Eton jacket down the toilet, frantically pulling the lever." I love my mother's version; she gets so into it she doesn't realize she's mimicking my movements and switching tenses. "But the damn jacket won't go down. You're working so hard you don't even hear me come in. Your face is beet red, there's water all over the floor and your little arm was half-way down the toilet."

"What did you do, Mummy?" I ask the same questions every time; it's all part of the reenactment.

"Well, I grabbed your arm and pulled you away, dear."

"What did I say?"

"You said, 'I want to wear a jacket with a collar.' That's when I decided it was time for you to go away to school."

"Only babies wear jackets without collars," I say.

My mother laughs, "Children don't notice clothes; they just wear them. I'll never understand why you were in such a hurry to get rid of that nice Eton jacket. Marched straight through the living room and up the stairs—without so much as a word."

It's one of those ritualistic memories that get blown up to family myth, almost as if my mother is talking about someone else. And yet, although I don't remember the incident like a teenager remembers his first kiss, it fits. It's the first manifestation of me being I. Perhaps some kid said something about my jacket. Perhaps I made it up because my father wore jackets with collars and I wanted to be like him. In any case, it's the reason I got sent to boarding school at the age of five.

•   •   •

I have another memory. Two years later. I'm in the Fetterden School locker room. The usual after-football-practice routine. Taking showers, getting dressed, a lot of yelling and roughhousing. Four of us in a tight circle, snapping towels at each other's private parts. My towel is heavy from the puddle of water it's been lying in. Its sting will be extra painful.

I'm dodging attackers on all sides. I duck a blow at my backside just as a shot to my ribs lands harmlessly. An instant's respite, a split second for my counter. *Thwack!* I can tell from the snap sound I've landed an elimination blow. The victim howls in pain and falls to the ground in a lump. *One down, two to go.* Outraged by the viciousness of my blow, the pack turns on me.

Pursued by six angry, towel-waving boys, I run out of the locker room. In my rush to escape, I slip and crash into the wall. I'm squatting down, examining my ankle, when my teammates come up. As soon as they see the blood oozing out, they head back to the locker room, as if to say, "Serves you right." My ankle is numb and already starting to swell. I look at the baseboard. A sliver of wood about three inches in length is missing. At that instant, I know the missing shard of baseboard molding is lodged in my foot from heel to toe. I'm quite familiar with the story of Achilles. *Perhaps, if I keep quiet I won't suffer his fate.*

I limp back to the deserted locker room, lift my foot to the sink and wash the wound with cold water. Then I dress myself and hobble to the toilet, leaving a trail of red drops across the gray linoleum floor. I stuff toilet paper into my sock to soak up the excess blood, wipe up my bloody tracks, and head to the infirmary.

On my way to the infirmary, I make the most important decision of my life. For reasons known only to a seven-year-old, I decide not to tell anyone about the splinter in my foot. In retrospect, I can't remember exactly why I refused to tell. Did I really believe the Achilles myth? It's too long ago and too muddled. But I do remember a particular fear of splinters. Perhaps, it was the way my mother always extracted them, slitting the skin with a razor blade, or poking at them with a needle in order to expose a tip to grip with the tweezers. And as deep as this splinter was, I knew it would hurt. Perhaps, it was a ploy to force my mother to remove me from boarding school.

So even under tough questioning by the nurse, I refuse to disclose its presence.

After she bandages me, I limp back to the dorm. The next morning the foot of the bed is soaked with blood. I go back to the infirmary. The nurse changes the bandage. That day I stay in the infirmary and, when my blood refuses to coagulate, the nurse gets anxious. A doctor examines me. That evening the doctor calls my mother in New York.

The next day I'm on a train to New York with the nurse. My mother meets us with an ambulance and off we go to Doctor's Hospital. That's when things get murky. All I remember is the doctors—the best pathologists and specialists in New York—can't find the splinter. I know it sounds amazing. But since I never say anything, it remains there, packed away in my foot.

Later on, long after the incident, my mother explains that wood doesn't show up in X-rays or in the fluoroscope[8] machines they used at the time. It doesn't sound credible to me, but what do I know?

My condition becomes critical. I go into a kind of comatose state, receiving blood transfusions and penicillin injections every four hours. Still I refuse to tell. And because the wound won't heal, pus oozes from my ankle and I have to be helped to the bathroom. Eventually, I am unable to go by myself. Attached to feeding and evacuation tubes, I lie in bed unaware of what is going on.

My mother is frantic. She harasses the doctors who are doing the best they can. Of course, my refusal to talk doesn't help; it makes them suspicious. They pressure my mother. I have a vague recollection of confessing to my mother, but only after swearing her to secrecy, making her take an oath never to tell anyone. Given my confused state, even today I don't remember whether I really told her.

I often wonder if that's why I was sent to Florida to live with my father and stepmother. Perhaps, it was my mother's way of keeping our confidence and taking care of the splinter at the same time. But if that's what really happened, it cost her dearly in the never-ending game of parental politics that divorced spouses play.

• • •

I wake up in a Florida state of mind. Almost by the fact of being in sunny Hobe Sound, the wound heals over. That's when I kind of snap back, about three months in all before I stop being delirious. Sealed inside, the splinter no longer bothers me. I resume walking without pain.

My father puts me in the one-room schoolhouse right on the beach. It's the only school I ever liked. I don't have to make much of an effort; I've already done the work at boarding school. In fact, I am so far ahead, I pass the time watching the girls. It's my first exposure to the opposite sex. Boarding schools in the 40s weren't co-ed.

Of course, the splinter's still lodged in my foot, and unbeknownst to me, wreaking havoc with vital nerve conduits. Visits to the local doctor are routine, until the day Dr. Larson announces, "There's a splinter in your foot."

"A splinter?" I exclaim, feigning surprise.

"Wood always works its way out. We can see it now."

"I don't know how those New *Yawk* bozos missed it," says my father. "The money your mother wasted. Don't you remember it going in?" My father's always suspected I was hiding something, but by this time, I'm an expert at deflecting his questions.

"No, Dad. I was running from these boys. I never saw anything. Guess it broke off inside. I didn't know wood worked its way out."

"Well, it does and I'm going to take it out," says the doctor. "The nurse will give you something. A few days and you'll be back in the water. In fact, salt water should do it good."

The nurse walks toward me, holding a mask. The next thing I know, the doctor is standing over me, shaking a jar of liquid with a fat three-inch splinter inside.

"You want it?" he asks.

Groggily, I look at it. "No," I say, turning toward my father.

"Bet you feel a couple of pounds lighter," he says.

• • •

A few months later, I ask my father if we can go to a movie, the new John Wayne western.

"We can see it tomorrow before you go back up North," he replies.

"Back up North?"

"You've been down here six months. You're behind. Keep it up and you won't get into Yale."

"I really like this school, Dad."

"You like the girls, you mean," says my stepmother.

"You need a good school, back East," says my father. "With team sports and accreditation."

"School's fun here…"

"School's not meant to be fun. You didn't think you were going stay here forever, become a plumber and live on a boat, did you?"

2—Consequences

Can we deny the fact that whether a fortuitous gift, divine grace, or the fruit of Karma, in every case there is a close link between the talent or beauty exhibited and the organic structure of the individual.

~ *The Awakening of Kundalini*—Gopi Krishna

M y mother and stepfather drive me to the Hersey School for Boys in Westchester County. I am nine years old, a fourth grader and already a veteran boarder. I'm resigned to it. All part of belonging to the eastern Brahmin establishment, says my 19-year-old cousin. When I tell him about the school in Florida, he laughs, tells me St. Paul's or Andover is where boys in our family go to school.

"You're lucky to be going to the best schools," says my father.

Well, my new school does seem less impersonal than Fetterden, and the headmaster projects a friendly attitude of concern. So after a few months I forget the school in Florida and throw myself back into the competition of sports, studies and other activities. With two exceptions.

Home for Christmas vacation, I tell my mother, "I forgot how to do math."

"Nonsense, you're just out of practice, dear," she replies.

"No," I insist, "I can't move the numbers around in my head any more."

"That Florida school was much too easy. You missed half a year of math."

"I used to be able to do problems in my head."

My mother's explanation sounds plausible, but I know she doesn't understand. I actually have forgotten how to do math. All of a sudden it's a grind. Problems I solved in my head in the third grade are like tangles of spaghetti. Rules I understood so easily and my ability to apply them have evaporated. Now numbers are, well, just numbers. Like in the way everyone else learns, by memorizing. That's it! Just to get by, I have to memorize. I can no longer calculate in my head. Okay, I've been in a fog for seven months, but that doesn't explain what's happened. Of course, no one pays attention. I don't dare tell my father. He'd say I'm not working hard enough. It's easy for my parents to explain the lapse. For all practical purposes, I missed a year of school.

It should have been a warning. After all, who knows more about my capabilities than me? But even if my parents had believed me, what could have been done to remediate the situation? Tutoring?

"That isn't necessary," says my mother. She thinks I'm a child prodigy.

Schools like mine have the best teachers. I'll catch up over time, she says. In the end, I probably would have accepted my mother's explanation if it hadn't been for yet another sign.

At the Fetterden school I sang in the choir. I had an amazing voice. Whenever I sang as a soloist, everyone, including my fellow choir members, turned to look. I loved to sing and was proud of my voice.

Although we don't have a choir in my new school, we sing popular songs like, "Home on the Range" and "Jimmy Crack Corn" at Friday night assemblies, and before Christmas vacation, carols and holy songs. The first time I sing with my new schoolmates, I notice that no one pays attention. This puzzles me. Then I notice I'm having trouble controlling my voice. Previously, I pitched my voice by placing it in various parts of my body and controlled the dynamics by using my breath to regulate the flow of air. In fact, I had an endless supply of breath. Yet, by the end of the first year at the Hersey School, not only am I struggling with math, I'm singing off key. Again, I tell my mother. But this time I have nothing to go on because, aside from humming around the house, I've been away at boarding school so much my mother has never heard me sing in performance.

What would you do if your nine-year-old child came home one day announcing that he had forgotten how to sing and do math? The same as my parents, I'll warrant. They didn't take me seriously. So I end up pushing the warning signs away.

By the time I start fifth grade, I've accepted my mother's explanation completely. Still, in the back of my mind, I know I once possessed these gifts. But what good is it to wonder? There's no practical way to get them back. I certainly don't believe hard work will do it. If anything, I feel cheated, a victim of some goofy hoax. Nothing in the entire universe can be done. I am growing in another direction, away from my lost abilities. And although that realization slowly slips beneath the surface, returning from time to time to shape the ways I think about myself, generally I just plain forget, burying my loss away in the lower layers of consciousness.

Much later, I came to discover the relationship between my accident and my lost abilities in math and singing. At the time though, I certainly didn't know about Pythagoras and his idea that math and music are related to harmony and physical symmetry. In fact, Pythagoras formed a cult around the idea that we are harmonically symmetrical beings. To Pythagoras, the structure of the body and musical harmony were contained in a mathematical expression. If one string was out of tune, the whole instrument played false. *We* are the instruments. And while the splinter was trapped inside my foot I lost that inner harmony. I started to shrivel. Like acupuncture in reverse, the splinter blocked a network of neural passages, altering my growth. Not only did it smother my talents, it sealed off parts of my memory.

If it hadn't been for those two indicators, I probably would have permanently accepted my mother's explanation. But my sudden inability at music and math were like waveform monitors—feedback on the altered state of my being. Sadly, no one around me at the time was capable of analyzing this feedback. Nevertheless, deep inside I retained a faint recollection of my lost abilities.

So why didn't I tell my mother about the splinter? The question still haunts me. It shows that, youth or adult, we are responsible for our acts. That a foreign stimulus entering the body can alter growth. That the merest slip of courage comes back to haunt us. That at every moment, even as children, we are called to face the consequences of our actions.

There were other signs, too. At seven I was a good tennis player, able to rally with my hard-hitting father, an amateur club champion wherever he played. When I next play with him, I still have excellent form, but I'm erratic. I can't control the ball. I was better at seven than at ten. The same explanations, the same rationalizations. Nevertheless, the fact that I no longer have anything to excel at influences my feelings about myself. And I begin to adjust my persona accordingly.

3—Stumbling

As Primal Spirit the life of man receives its human nature from father and mother. This Primal Spirit is without consciousness and knowledge, but is able to regulate the formative processes of the body.

At the time of birth the Conscious Spirit inhales the energy and thus becomes the dwelling of the new-born. It lives in the heart. From that time on the heart is master, and the Primal Spirit loses its place while the Conscious Spirit has the power.[9]

> ~ *The Secret of the Golden Flower*—Lu Yen - Richard Wilhelm, Translator

As I grow, my body stretches and my face flattens, as if crushed from the side by a hydraulic press. My nose becomes elongated, my eyes close together. I am not un-athletic, but I am not the confident young math student, singer, and tennis player of an earlier time. I am slender, almost gaunt with no natural muscular tone. Before the accident I had a large round head. I often look at the portrait my mother had taken before my accident and wonder what happened.

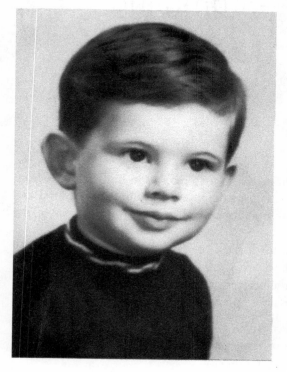

Figure 1: I'm 2 years old

Of course, I understand how the body morphs as we age. But it doesn't seem possible that the *Me* in the portrait should become the 14-year-old boy about to enter high school.

The changes aren't just physical. I'm a daydreamer who avoids and puts off every task. I don't excel—not at sports or studies. Yet, at no time am I aware—as I am today—that my body, and consequently my being, are victims of my decision not to tell the school nurse about the splinter.

My growth takes a detour. I'm not talking about the adjustments that go with adolescence. Without knowing it, I am becoming a different being. I begin to fashion an altered persona to match my altered body. I guess you could say that some watchdog process inside me is constantly evaluating my appearance and fashioning a persona—a mode of behavior—to go with it. I become the class clown. Disrupting moves the class along. I don't have to work as hard. I toggle between two states: class clown and daydreamer.

Now, I don't wake up one day and say: *Hey, my body's not growing the way it should. Yikes, I'm metamorphosizing! I know…I'll adjust my behavior. That way no one will notice because I'll be acting the way this new sort of person usually acts.* No, it isn't a conscious effort; it's a protective mechanism, a means of allowing my altered being to fit into my surroundings. And in boarding school fitting in is essential.

As I write, I realize it's almost impossible to imagine. First, you—the reader—have to accept that because of the splinter, my physical growth took a detour. Next, you must accept that, at some level, I was aware of it and, in order to fit in, I fashioned a new persona on the fly. It's easy to say: *he only imagined it, it couldn't have happened. The only proof he gives us is a vague impression that he forgot how to do math. That's not much.*

It's not much? It's everything. It's the empirical truth of the body. Our beings are always talking to us through our bodies. Every time some outside agent, self-induced or not, hurts our bodies, our bodies speak to us.

You don't think your body talks to you when you drink too much? So maybe you don't drink. I'll substitute something else. My first cigarette. It wasn't pleasant. In fact, inhaling was downright excruciating. Hiding in the woods while two older boys lit me up. The hacking and coughing. Their laughing at my misery.

"You want to throw up," they say. "A few more tokes and you won't."

Right then and there, I might have listened to my body. But I didn't. Why not? Because the mind made it possible for me to take the self-abuse. The mind rationalized my discomfort, and made *fitting in* a more important value than protecting my body.

The MIND—the great rationalizer—is constantly at war with the body. And where do those comforting rationalizations originate? Do they come from within, from our beings? No, the mind absorbs them from the culture. *My best friend smokes Camels, maybe I should switch…Don't be a dope, Sarah, just because your parents are uptight about sex doesn't mean you have to be…It's Miller time. Look at those hotties. Have another beer, Tim, and we'll go get a tattoo. That's something the babes really go for.*

You see, the mind and the body really aren't friends. The mind is a tool of the culture, an expert propagandist for *fitting in*. Yet, as the mind drowns out the truth, the body continues to tell it. Which is your real friend? The body, you say. Do you listen to it? I didn't.

And yet, at some level, I must have. I never would have made it back otherwise. Spiraling out control, there has to be some measure of omniscience, or else recovery is impossible. The mind is just too strong. It campaigns incessantly for all the things you think you ought to be doing, all the things you think you are missing. How can you possibly stand up to the supplications of the mind?

Nevertheless, as my abilities decline and the memory of my accident fades, I keep a sense of awareness in spite of the things my new persona tells me about myself. Without it, I would never have found a way to restore myself—for the worst is yet to come.

4—Failure

Even the most piddling life is of momentous consequence to its owner.

~ James Wolcott

In the 1950s, my New England prep school—yet another boarding school—is a place of such privilege that failure to gain entry
to a prestigious university is almost unheard of. *Stagger into the
interview with the Ivy League recruiters. Act respectfully. Share a few
nods and winks. Answer a few perfunctory questions. C average? No
problem. Mediocre SATs? We can work things out. Need a scholarship?
Hey, we like your family tree.*

Although I never recover my exceptional ability at math, by
my senior year I've memorized the operations. Connecticut boarding schools like Woolley make it difficult to fail. The teachers are
great and second chances are plentiful. In fact, the system hates
failure. Get along and you are almost guaranteed entry into some
Ivy-adorned campus. By my senior year, I am an expert at conning
the system. After all, I've been at boarding school for twelve years.
Hovering between a B and a D, I do just enough to keep my parents
satisfied. In spite of my resentment toward being sent away, I have to
keep them believing I am clever.

At age 15, I drift away from math as a favorite subject. I
become an avid reader with a fresh sense of curiosity. My favorites
are James Joyce and Aldous Huxley, twin rages of the 50s. With
their seminal books under my belt, I feel prepared for discussions on
existentialism, nihilism and the meaning of life. To strengthen my
reshaped persona, I adopt a lot of big words. Substituting literature
for math isn't so much of a love of literature as a defense mechanism.
*Math skills declining? Gotta have a substitute? Voilà Lit! The perfect
replacement!* After all, math is black and white; you either know the
answer or you don't. With Lit, if you write 15 pages, no one will
know the difference as long as you use a lot of big words, or so I
thought.

It's not that I'm not serious about Lit; my curiosity is genuine.
I just don't know what I am talking about most of the time. So it's a
big blow to my newfound persona of intellectual when I receive my
senior report card. In it, the headmaster summarizes my career in
these words: "This boy has no talent."

This upsets my mother and stepfather, of course. They rather
approve of my new persona. In fact, their first impulse is to defend
me. When I read my report card, I'm puzzled, and a bit indignant. I

don't have much to do with the headmaster. How dare he say I have no talent! He never speaks to me, but somehow he's pegged me.

I have to admit I squandered the fall term. Doing what exactly? Well, while everyone in my senior dorm was reading *The Scarlet Letter* or studying math and history, I slipped into the corridor to catch flies with my hands. The human spider, I stalked the halls, running up my nightly total of flies. I became good at it. It's difficult to look back, to watch myself waste a school term at such a useless pastime.

Roper, my roommate, tries to reason with me. "What the hell are you doing?" he asks.

"Perfecting a hand-eye coordination technique," I reply.

"They'll have you back in study hall with a D average, you know."

I couldn't answer him then. Now I know why. It had been about ten years since the splinter incident. Uninterrupted physical growth is linear, but a negative stimulus causes the body to implode, creating a gap between intended and actual physical symmetry. The splinter was just such a negative stimuli.

Comparison between Interrupted and Uninterrupted Growth

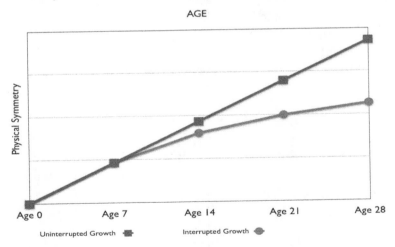

Because of it, my symmetry takes a new direction at age seven. From that moment on, it begins to sag. That's right—it isn't even a straight-line deviation; it's a downward curve. Why? Over time, the gap widens geometrically. By age 28, the gap between my intended and actual symmetry will be greater than the gap at age 14. The gap is a compilation of physical, mental, emotional, psychological and spiritual growth. They're all intertwined, all dependent on physical symmetry. So unless I find a way to close the gap, the curve will spiral downward with the last remnants of my mortal being.

Unaware of this, I rationalize my predicament in terms of the situation at hand. It comes out something like this: College is a lock, so why study? The truth is, I am lost in an inner turmoil bounded by inertia—a kind of living nothing. My grades nosedive.

As Roper predicted, I'm put back in study hall. A senior in study hall is unheard of. I shrink down in my chair while everyone stares and whispers. Still, I refuse to study. As soon as the monitor passes by, I open the book hidden inside my bag. Somerset Maugham, DH Lawrence, Orwell, Camus, Conrad and Fitzgerald are my favorites.

My parents discuss changing schools. Perversely, I resist. When they ask me why, I dodge the question. But I'm more honest with myself, even if I don't do anything about it. The truth hurts, especially the headmaster's remark about my lack of talent. Not enough to make me try, not in the traditional sense, not in my studies. Yet I wonder why I can't excel at anything. Hell, I don't even understand the books I'm reading. Okay, maybe at some level they influence me. But for the most part, I'm pretending. Desperately trying to be someone.

• • •

I meet Roper, my Woolley School roommate, at a friend's house, Cecil Hesse, heir to a cosmetic fortune. Roper and Cecil were roommates at Springer Academy before Roper got kicked out for drinking and Cecil skipped his junior year to go straight to Columbia. Cecil is a genius, Roper explains.

Cecil and his father, Eric, live in a three-story Eastside brownstone. Eric Hesse is tall, erect and Jewish. His goatee reminds me of an Aldous Huxley hero. Cecil is a younger version with a rounder face. Neither the younger nor the elder Hesse dresses preppy like

Roper or me. They wear turtlenecks and rubbed leather suede shoes, all conceived with a certain Bauhaus look: sleek yet expensive. Both are sophisticated and have deep voices that radiate gravitas. Their clothes make me aware of my parochial limitations. I feel like sneaking off to the toilet and flushing down my entire wardrobe. I have never been exposed to life outside my family's circle of WASP friends. I am in awe of Eric Hesse.

The coldest Christmas vacation in memory, I dread the thought of standing on Lexington Avenue hailing a downtown cab. That's when Cecil persuades his father to drop us. But on the drive downtown, Eric Hesse insists on stopping at the Biltmore Bar. Three large tumblers are placed before us: *Rémy Martin, Hennessy, Courvoisier*. Eric asks us if we can tell one from another, like this might be a parlor game I played with my parents. I'm flattered that someone is treating me like an adult—all the more reason to admire Eric Hesse. In the end, only Cecil, of course, passes the taste-test. When it's my turn I have enough trouble swallowing the fiery liquid, much less making an educated guess.

"*L'appétit vient en mangeant,*"[10] exclaims Eric Hesse, slapping me on the back. I gulp it down to everyone's amusement.

Three new tumblers appear. Somehow I am able to identify the Courvoisier. With each swallow I try not to betray the marinated-in-kerosene sensation chafing my throat. At half-empty, I forget about my throat altogether. I laugh at Cecil and Eric's elegant banter soaking up stories of famous writers and artists, even contributing my own *bons mots* from time to time. And from the looks on their faces, not behaving too ridiculously. Encouraged by their nods and winks, I launch forth on my own, not like at school, trying to impress Mrs. Flanagan, the history instructor's wife. No, I'm soaring, floating above the conversation, giving tongue to a world of new ideas. Yes, a Brave New World is opening up for me, as if I've broken away from the limited world of my parents. I've read Somerset Maugham and DH Lawrence and now I am standing beside Huxley's 'Complete Rabelaisian Man.'

Or so it seems. Must be the Cognac. I can't see myself thrashing and lurching around in the back of the car on the way to the Café Bohemia. My attention is everywhere at once: thoughts of the Biltmore bar, visions of a Bohemian life, the lights on Second Avenue, Mrs. Flanagan's velvety white throat. My mind is like a crab claw, snapping at anything that moves.

"You all right, man?" asks Cecil.

"Yeah."

"Just so you are…" Cecil stares at me, as if he is having second thoughts about introducing me into a sacred brotherhood. *Like, what if I barf on the customers? Hesse's own standing might plummet.*

Talk about mood altering, it's like going from a casino to a church. One minute I am using liquefied energy to propel myself to the pinnacle of self-expression, the next I am in a cavern surrounded by a hush so moodful that the world seems to be teetering between slow motion and inertia. Glasses clink, chiaroscuro people at small round tables whisper breathlessly. Cocktail waitresses in short white aprons scuttle between the tiny tables delivering drinks and collecting money. Behind them at the bar, stick figures lounge in various poses from tight to languid. A young black man in an Ivy League suit appears on the stage carrying a cymbal, which he tightens onto the top of a tripod. He sits behind his drum set and ruffles a few rolls. A few ears prick up.

A long-legged black girl in a waitress costume takes our order. Three more men, one white, appear on the bandstand. The white guy picks up a saxophone; the other two slither in behind bass and piano respectively. The tinkling stops. All eyes swing to the curtain.

Onto the small stage steps a tensile young black man in a more expensive Ivy League suit. The sidemen ready themselves as the leader fingers his trumpet valves. Mouthpiece to his lips, he raises his elbows. When he brings them down, the music explodes and Eric Hesse is forgotten, replaced by Miles Davis. Perfect anti-hero for the fifties: *blacks, bohemians, beatniks, students, outsiders.*

When he finishes his solo, Miles walks to a corner of the stage, turns his back on the audience. JR Montrose, the tenorman, is deep in his solo, but I am watching Miles. He breaks off a noiseless riff, turns and walks to the piano, puts his foot on the bench, and just listens. It's the first time I've heard jazz—not just some watered-down Broadway jazz—the Prince of Darkness himself. It's perfect, beyond words; the most exalted expression of feeling I've ever encountered.

Afterwards, I puke my guts out on Sheridan Square. Hesse takes pity on me, leads me to an all-night record store on Broadway, where under his expert guidance, I buy some Charlie Parker, Miles Davis, Sonny Rollins and Dave Brubeck 10" LPs. Some are chosen for the originality of the cover art. Brooding, melancholy Art Pepper—even Hesse has never heard of him—but the cover art conveys a kind of existential yearning. Here is someone who had found his own level and excelled at it.

I take the lot back to my dormitory at the Woolley School and listen over and over to the esoteric music that no one else can stand. I imagine myself a hero in a modern Faustian allegory: being able to trade my soul for something to excel at.

It certainly isn't ice hockey. I'm the weakest skater on the team, so they stick me in the goal. I hate the pucks whizzing around my head. I hate the fact that I duck each time a puck flies toward me. I must be lucky. The team is undefeated. All I remember are skates, sticks and bodies crashing into me, and my teammates congratulating me for the all pucks that somehow wind up in my glove.

None of the Woolley School faculty has ever played hockey and the school doesn't have the money to pay an outside coach. We ask Mr. Foster, the English teacher, to act as our unofficial coach and driver for the road games. He never comes to practice, so when his station wagon stops beside me as I walk to the dorm one night, it's instant panic.

"Get in," he says. "We're going to the Head's house." We drive off, listening to HV Kaltenborn on the car radio while I review a multitude of infractions that have never come to light.

"Anything the matter, boy?" asks Mr. Foster.

"No sir."

"How was practice?"

"Great, sir. You should come out once in a while."

"Too cold—if you don't carry one of those sticks," he says.

● ● ●

The way the headmaster looks at me, I feel like the ultimate cornered rat. Quickly, I review my backlog of infractions. *But no, he takes out his Bible. Gotta be something else. He never uses the Bible for castigating sin. It's not Episcopalian.*

Mrs. Flanagan comes in, smiles at me, and whispers in the headmaster's ear. The Head rises and shuffles toward the vestibule to a figure standing in the shadows. *Mister Semple* is the only part of the conversation I catch.

Uh-oh, I've been kicked out. My father's come to take me away. No, wait a minute, those faces are telling me something. What, goddamn it?

How do I take the news of my mother's death? I don't cry. Perhaps I cried too much when I went away to school at the age of five. There are no tears left. All that manly Spartan, old-school crap. *Come back with your shield or on it!*

All I can think about when my father shows up is I'm getting kicked out. I never, ever thought of this. The only person I could talk to and she sent me away to school when I was five. She had a channel into me, into who I am. And now she's dead.

On the way from Metcalf, Connecticut to New York City, my father hardly speaks. He tells me the story on the way out of the school driveway. "She fell down the stairs," he says. "We'll get the details in the city."

I look at him in stunned disbelief. "What happened?"

Then he lets me have it. "They think she was dead by the time she reached the bottom. That's all I know."

"Fell down the stairs? Dead?"

"We're going to the funeral home. Ben's there. I don't know any more because Ben was so upset on the phone."

After that exchange my father doesn't say another word for two and a half hours, not until we pull in front of a Lexington Avenue funeral parlor and I see my mother lying in a casket.

All during the drive I think about my mother. It isn't the time for tears, not with my father sternly bearing down on the road and my stomach churning. The winding road has me on the verge of puking. I refuse to ask him to pull over. Instead, I think about my mother telling me that I'd make a fine Episcopal minister.

"That's because you don't think I can do anything else. So, I need to stay out of the way of the world in some quiet corner and gather my flock."

"I didn't say that, dear. You're a deep boy who just needs time."

Yeah, time…time to figure out why there is nothing I excel at. Nothing I do well. No talent. No skill.

"Here we are," says my father pulling up behind a line of hearses.

I don't want to see her body; I don't want to remember her that way. Just lying there dead. My mother, the first dead person I've ever seen! What a sheltered fuck I've been. I know it's probably wrong, not wanting to see her, but what good does it do? Dead is dead. While everyone, with the exception of my father—and I respect him for it—is muttering platitudes about how peaceful she looks, I can only say to myself, 'That's not my mother. What there was of her is not there in that casket.'

Ben Peck, my stepfather, is dazed—a grief-stricken, lost soul. I wonder how he'll survive. Contrast Ben's reckless emotion with my father's discomfort. When Ben embraces me, I burst into tears for a moment, quickly trying to control myself. *For my own sake, or my father's? I'm not quite sure.*

Later on in the car, I ask my father if I can continue to see Ben. The question doesn't sit well. He's jealous of the other man's easy sense of intimacy. *All of my things are at my mother's apartment. Will I ever see them again?* It seems to me that before my eyes at my mother's funeral, a wordless protocol deciding my future is thrashed out and I have no say in it.

My mother was the only person I'd told about the connection between the splinter and my lost abilities. She never probed or questioned me, like a psychologist might do, but I know she sensed something.

5—Disintegration

There are 8 million stories in the Naked City. This is one of them.

~ *The Naked City*—Mark Hellinger-Producer

The day my father drives me to matriculate at the University of Pennsylvania, he gives me a checkbook with a $1000 account. His last words are, "Make this last until Christmas."

Okay, so I didn't make it to Yale, but Penn's not bad. An Ivy League school in a big city. And Philadelphia's a lot more fun than New Haven. Even though there's a slight sense of letdown—that I've disappointed my family once again—I'm at the top of my game.

A thousand dollars is a lot in September of 1956. I spend it in two weeks. It isn't difficult. Although I have a room in the dorms and meals in the dining hall, I fall in with some cool dudes at a fraternity house—young men from the best prep schools. While the rules forbid freshmen from living at a frat house, my companions make an exception. Perhaps it's the drinks I'm always buying. Maybe it's my stooge-like behavior. It might even be the money I lose at bridge and poker. I remind myself of one of those profligate, fallen aristocrats in an Oscar Wilde play. But the difference between my prospective frat brothers and myself is, that in spite of the hard drinking and gambling, they stay up half the night studying. I, on the other hand, explore the Philadelphia demimonde by night: jazz clubs, dance halls, all-night movies, bars.

When my money runs out, I don't have a choice. My mother isn't around to be wheedled, so I call my father in New York. Tersely, he announces the solution: a check for seven dollars in the mail each week, then he hangs up. That should have lit a fire, but it didn't. The day I receive the check, the seven dollars are gone. The rest of the week, I scrounge.

I affect an eccentric personality. During the long Philadelphia winter I wear a black Chesterfield overcoat with a frayed velvet collar, and white tennis shoes with no socks. I'm never sick; I'm too busy asserting my freedom from boarding school. I imagine myself an artist. I possess all the artistic sensibilities but no talent. That will come, I tell myself. I'll become a writer later on; for the moment I'm observing life.

Fortunately, the frat house lets me eat on credit. As long as I eat, I'll survive. I buy a 1945 Ford for $25. I am one of the most colorful characters on campus. Everybody says so. That makes it easy to skip class.

Finally, come June, the day of reckoning, my father tells me I have to take my butt—torn Chesterfield and all—into the Armed Forces. Once again, it should have had an impact. Somewhere inside, I should have said to myself, "Hey, man, wake up. Get back to college and apply yourself." Yet, meekly, I acquiesce.

I find myself at Parris Island. I don't fall over on the long marches. Nor does my rifle come apart during inspection. Mostly, I stay out of trouble. This is serious business, after all. One false move and into the brig. Like the boarding school friend I run across at the Episcopal Chapel. Instead of the normal 12 weeks, he's been on the Island for 22 weeks, part of that time in the brig. When we meet, he's set for a long run. They've told him he'll stay until he gets his weight down. I've never seen a man so miserable. Depressed, nearly suicidal, soon he's weeping on my shoulder. *There but for the grace of God go I.* It makes me dread institutions even more.

When I land permanent duty at Camp Lejeune, I'm determined to get back to civilization. Bivouacking on the mosquito-infested beaches is no place to spend the next eighteen months.

My only escape? The town of Jacksonville, North Carolina, a provincial backwater of epic proportions. Beside hockshops and sleazy bars, there's nothing except the movie emporium, the place I spend my weekends.

One Saturday, before the show, a black friend and I are turned away from Howard Johnson's. "I can't serve you in here with him," says the waitress.

"What do you mean?" I ask. At that moment we are just two hungry customers. I'm not expecting racism. But then I'm not black.

"We can't serve you with him, sir," repeats the waitress.

Then the manager comes bounding up. And I tell Jackson I'll speak to him—after all, we're in uniform. I picture myself standing up to injustice, smoothing things over, just like my mother used to do in fancy New York restaurants. Jackson is wiser; he knows about southern intransigence.

"Forget it," he says.

We go to a darktown café on the other side of town. On the jukebox Sarah Vaughan is singing "The Nearness of You." A deep sense of comfort sweeps over me as we sit discussing politics, boxing and jazz music while eating fish and greens. I have to find a way out.

When the Marine Corps sees a year of college on my record, they arrange for me to take the Officer Candidate test. Here's my out. Then it hits me. I don't want to be an officer. I won't be able to order anyone around, much less the kind of guys in my unit. They won't respect me. Hell, I don't even respect myself. I have to get back to a life I can disappear into.

A kind of junior grade SAT, I don't even pass the test for OCS. I've slipped so low in cognitive skills that even my prep school education—Latin, trigonometry, calculus, French, literature—doesn't help. A distinguished prep school plus one year at an Ivy League University, and I still can't pass. My failure is a protest against boredom, I tell myself. I could have passed if I'd really wanted to. *I have no idea that the splinter has damaged my cognitive abilities to such an extent. I am disintegrating.*

Finally, to get an assignment in Washington, DC, I enlist for a third year. Anything is better than Camp Lejeune, North Carolina.

There aren't enough bunks at the Marine Barracks on 8th and I Streets so the lucky ones like myself are given a housing allowance and told to find apartments. Ironically, my work at the Navy Yard involves math; I have to teach it. Through the teaching of algebra, geometry and trigonometry by correspondence to Marines all over the world, I find I'm able to master the ability to teach. I pride myself on breaking down the concepts for the Marines in the field. They haven't had the education I've had, yet I envy them. They have something to work for, and potentially, something to excel at.

When I get out of the Marine Corps, I enroll at George Washington University. In 1960, drugs are a timely addition to my vices. I have them all: booze, sex, bad eating habits and now drugs.

Am I a better student? Not really. I'm not interested in anything except literature, although I do attend classes for a change. Mainly, the university is the place to meet girls. As for a clear vision of my future, there just doesn't seem to be one. I take a writing course, and although the teacher encourages me, I find the work tedious. He keeps telling me I have the makings of a good writer. Perhaps it's all the big words I learned at boarding school, I tell him. I disappear into Bohemia after dark.

I work odd jobs: store detective, carpenter, caddy. When I get the lead in a play written by a friend of mine, I quit my job. My new calling is acting. I am high on booze or drugs for rehearsals and performances. During the final cast party, my friend tells me he gave me the part because he couldn't find anyone else. For 45 straight minutes he talks while I smile and listen. I'm so stoned I think we are having a deep intellectual discussion, only to finally figure out he's been telling me how bad an actor I am. Not that it bothers me; I can rationalize anything. I certainly don't have a clear idea of what it takes to be an actor.

I don't realize it, but some craving is pushing me to reach for something to excel at. First, it's literature, now acting. But each time I latch onto something substantial, I fail at it.

I meet a French woman. Like most of the women in my life, Madeleine is exceptional. I've witnessed a lot of screwed-up relationships. I guess I'm lucky; the women I meet seem to operate on a higher plane. Madeleine doesn't care about my lack of ambition. She supports my curiosity. It's almost as if she's been put here to help me find myself, to take up the slack left by my mother's death. We move in together. I finish the semester poorly, with the exception of my writing course. I quit school and get a job. Without a college degree, Madeleine tells me, I have to find some high-paying job skill or I'll be a low wage slave forever. After two years in a drug store film lab, I talk my way into a motion picture lab. Film becomes my new passion.

• • •

"I must have missed the last part, what were you saying?" With Madeleine at my bedside, I'm dozing after an appendicitis operation.

"Nothing, *chéri*," she says.

"Tell me, I want to hear," I say.

"Moving to London so you could go to the London Film School."

"Oh." I drift off again, then wake with a shudder. "They gave me morphine. Three nights in a row. I'm still a bit groggy."

"I don't like opiates. What was it like?"

"Like nothing else. Uh, maybe like pot a bit, or an acid trance. But instead of being an observer, I was actor *and* observer. Like I've been under water my whole life, and for once I could see above it. Do you know what I mean?"

"No."

"Well, after the nurse shot me up, I was in this half-state between sleep and waking. A great glowing light filled the room. Suddenly, I was floating upward. When I reached the ceiling, I realized I could steer myself. I'm having trouble though. I command myself to roll over and I'm looking down at my physical body, asleep in the bed, and I realize that I'm in an altogether different body."

"So?"

"So I stayed up there watching my body asleep in the bed. I knew I could leave the room, but I didn't know if I'd be able to get back. I knew I'd see amazing things, but I figured I had to return to my body, that I wasn't ready to take off and leave it."

"Hummph."

"Well, it opened my mind... Perhaps, I shouldn't say 'mind' because the mind may not be part of it."

"Well, if it isn't the mind, what is it?"

"I don't know," I mumble.

"Roper's at Harvard Business School," she continues.

"Oh? No kidding. Business school."

"Yeah."

"Why?"

"Duh, because he's into business...like you're into film. Now's your chance to really learn it."

Later, when the night nurse comes in, I ask her for my morphine shot. Not tonight, she tells me, there's a three-night limit. I'm disappointed—no chance to fly over the city at night...

Madeleine and I talk about a lot of things. The London Film School. Immigrating to New Zealand. Buying a house. Not having kids. Madeleine doesn't want them; she wants to travel, live outside the United States. But we can't seem to make it happen. Heck, I drink too much, do too many drugs, play around, even on Madeleine. I keep talking about film school, but Madeleine's had enough talk.

Through my aunt, I find work as an assistant film editor at a major network. Washington is cheap in the sixties. We move into a big house on Macomb Street off Rock Creek Park and quickly fall into the party scene. Soon we have wannabes and bigwigs inviting us to bizarre parties every night. And even though we play at being close—treat each other as if we share some deep dark secrets—we are flirting with danger. Madeleine says that she doesn't see anything wrong with "seeing other people."

"Are you doing it?" I ask.

"No."

"But you think we could handle it."

Madeleine replies with an enigmatic smirk.

• • •

Madeleine comes in with a load of groceries, stacks the bags on the kitchen table. I have my foot up on the chair, staring at the inside front cover of *Anna Karenina.* She begins to load the groceries into the refrigerator.

"Oh," she says, startled, "I didn't see you there."

"I'm not really here."

"Don't be cryptic, *chéri.* I only have an hour and my mind's not on the kitchen yet."

"Nosing up a line or two should clear the cobwebs."

"Why don't you help me, instead of being so clever."

"Fine, what do you want me to do?"

"Well, they'll be here in an hour and a half. I have to cook all this—chicken, turnips, leeks, onions."

"I'll do it…" I say.

"You know how?"

"*Poule au Pot?* I've watched you use the *Cocotte Minute,*[11] you know."

"I've watched my dentist do a root canal. Doesn't mean I'm capable of doing one."

"Browning the vegetables and the chicken, the tablespoon of flour, the wine...adding leeks and all. I can taste it already."

"You really have been watching, *je crois!*"

I take the book into the bedroom and change my clothes. I intend to retreat there when Madeleine starts to sniff coke with Julian Fish. That's what I do every Friday when the Fishes come over. Only I get drunk and pass out, waking up about 3:30 a.m. with Denise Fish passed out alongside me. When I walk into the living room at 4:00 a.m., Julian and Madeleine go on talking as if I'm not there.

I suspect they are fucking, but never catch them, even when I tiptoe down the hall. I don't know about Denise. She's leggy and French, a model, with dark black hair, ostensibly a friend of Madeleine's. But it's really between Julian and Madeleine that the juices flow. Sure, Denise complements Julian's impeccably groomed demeanor. But I don't care. Neither about their fucking, if that's what they're up to, nor about waking up next to the beautiful Denise. I am losing my mind, paranoid that Madeleine's about to leave me.

Later after dinner I'm reading *Anna Karenina* when Denise comes in, looking startled.

"Surprised I'm not passed out?"

Denise giggles—or as close as the French come to giggling— then tosses back her immaculate hair.

"Don't you wonder what they do in there?" I ask.

"F*oo*cking. What did you expect?"

"Oh."

She laughs. "That's what we're supposed to do. Really they think you're such a loser. It's five times we come here and each time you pass out."

"Am I a loser if I don't really give a damn? I mean..." my voice starts to modulate into a scream, "I really don't give a fucking shit."

Denise shrugs, then sits down next to me on the bed.

"There is one thing, Denise."

"Yes?"

"How did you like my *Poule au Pot?* I mean compared to Madeleine's."

"R*eea*lly good," she laughs. "I wasn't k*ee*ding. The best I ever ate, no sh*ee*t."

"Uh...does my reading bother you?"

She shakes her head. "Would you like to make love? So I can tell Julian, I mean."

"If it's something that Julian gets a thrill out of—rehashing your carnal pleasures with other dudes—then no, sorry, I'd like to be excused."

"Let me take my clothes off, *au moins.*"

She stands up, strips in front of me, demurely turning her back, letting her clothes fall to the floor, trying to show me she's a classy chick—then she jumps into bed alongside me.

Well, I read all right—for about ten seconds. It's funny how difficult it is to keep your mind on your business with a luscious babe softly writhing under the sheets just inches away. I could smell her, hear her soft murmurs and enticements. We fuck—for about two straight hours. No drugs, nothing. There's something about Denise's hole and my cock that coincide perfectly. No shouting, no screaming, it builds and builds but never gets there. Always intense, all consuming, never coming. To this day I don't know what it is. The Perfect Fuck! I guess.

As we walk into the living room later on, Denise whispers, "I won't say anything to Julian, darl*ee*ng."

I'm dependent on Madeleine. I will never leave her. I'll let her leave me, if that's what she wants. I'll flay my skin, put on sackcloth and ashes. I'll let her leave. I'll make it easy for her.

So Madeleine is fucking Julian and Denise and I are supposed to follow suit. Well, two days later, Madeleine announces she is leaving me for Julian Fish.

What about Denise? I wonder. *Evidently, the distraught Denise is not thinking about other men right at the moment.* About all I can say is, "How am I going to find my socks?"

Madeleine doesn't dignify my question with an answer. I take another tack: "So, it's because Julian's rich and I'm not, right? Is he better at...you know, fucking? You know you love me, in spite of my faults, which are many and serious. We can see a counselor. We don't have to stay in DC. There're better places to live."

I probe, without response. She simply isn't *there* any more. Emotionally, she has slipped away and isn't coming back, ever.

She leaves most of her belongings at the house and moves into a friend's with Julian. We can't talk face-to-face because Julian surrounds her with all kinds of polite go-betweens, who speak of 'their love' as if they are Dante and Beatrice. It's so beautiful, blah, blah, blah. It's so beautiful because Julian has money, a trust fund from his parents, and they can tool around DC in his Jaguar.

What about our love? *Don't we have the London Film School?* When I mention it that night on the phone, Madeleine laughs, "Who wants to live in London?"

"But I thought…"

"That was just talk, like your morphine thing."

"You have a better place?"

"Julian and I are going to Mexico. You know how I've always wanted to live there."

"Un-huh."

Julian tells her to be afraid of me. Our every contact has to be over the phone. *Afraid of me?* She isn't afraid of me, she explains. "I *have* to leave."

Sounds preordained, like I'm up against forces greater than anything I've ever known. "What does 'have to leave' mean?" I ask. She's late; we can talk later.

Late for their ritual trip to the movies, to see "What's New, Pussycat?" They've seen it every night for a week. I'm numb, and the feeling is getting more intense. Just the thought of Tom Jones' voice makes me sick. We used to ball for hours to Billie Holiday and Monk. And now evidently, they are humping to "What's New, Pussycat?"

As for Denise, she's equally stunned. We agree that nothing can equal our one-night stand and there is no reason to spoil it. We like each other, Denise and I, but that has nothing to do with living together (those on-the-double-rebound things never work anyway). Although she's used to high-flyers like Julian, underneath she wants a simple life. Even my *Poule au Pot* isn't enough, she says. Anyway, I have things to do. One way or other, I'm going to the London Film School.

That's my plan. Instead, two nights later I get drunk and wait for Julian on a side street off Connecticut Avenue. I know he uses a parking lot there and walks to the apartment.

I crouch down behind a hedge, falling over backwards from time to time in a drunken sprawl. Once, I think I hear Julian talking to another man. I pop up just as two guys walk by. When they see me in my ripped condition, they take off. This makes me even bolder. I begin mumbling to myself as I tip from a pint of bourbon.

"He's so great, huh? Then why did Denise tell me about some Mexican penis rub he uses? Bad fuck is what. I'll tell you something else, Denise. Not everyone is everyone else's great fuck—like you an' me. It's like food. Not everyone likes broccoli, I know I did, but most kids don't...didn't. And not everyone can get comfortable with the same pussy. Where do you think we'd be if we cared more about 'the fuck' than 'the person,' bitch?"

Footsteps on 19th Street. My adrenaline takes over. I crouch down next to a hole in the hedge and listen as they get louder and closer. Low voices, too. Incoherent. Man and woman, or man talking to himself. I can't tell. *Click, clickity, click.*

When they reach the hole, I pop up. I watch Julian turn, looking surprised for a split second before I swing. I miss him and hit Madeleine instead, knocking her out. *Bap!* and she falls. Julian takes off running, then thinks better of it. I crouch down by the gate waiting for him. I am crazed and drunk, and I want to kill him. The gate opens and a very tentative Julian Fish enters. I'm up and on him, swinging. I knock him down and start clobbering him, banging his head on the pavement.

Out on the street, Madeleine is struggling to get up, crying "Julian, Julian." It should be my name she's bawling. I get up and run out of the yard like the mad fool that I am.

The next morning I wake with a headache, feeling vaguely guilty about something, something I can't quite recall. Then the phone rings and it all comes back. It's Julian. He sounds suspicious. Did I know they were mugged? "By who?" I ask. They were hiding behind a tree, so he didn't get a good look at them.

"Oh," I say. "They...there were two of them?" I want to confess, but not to Julian. And now that Madeleine has switched from Lady Day to Tom Jones, I don't feel I can get a fair shake from her.

"DC's not safe, we're going to Mexico."

"Mexico...Where in Mexico?"

"My father has a ranch. We can live there while I take pictures."

My plan has worked. They're going to Mexico. They'll disappear off the face of the earth and I'll go to London and become a film director. I certainly can't get any lower; I mean this is the bottom. Drunk, and beating up Madeleine on the street. Like a self-fulfilling prophecy, Julian told her to be afraid of me. I'm sure he made it up to stop her from seeing me, and yet I had to make it come true.

"Are you sure you don't know anything about it?" asks Julian.

"I'll keep my eyes and ears open. Can I talk to Madeleine?"

"She doesn't want to talk to anyone. She's too upset. We're not going to 'What's New, Pussycat?' tonight. Too much insanity."

I sit there wooly-headed and bewildered. The phone rings again and I think it might be Madeleine. My heart puffs like a soufflé, instantly deflating when I hear my boss's voice.

There's a new show starting and I have to meet the supervising editor.

"Yes," I reply. "Give me work, lots of work."

"It'll mean lots of money," he says.

"Good! I need money, lots of money."

That's the last I see of Julian and Madeleine. They fly to Mexico the next day. Only a chosen few know of their whereabouts. *Poof. My time is up; it's someone else's turn.*

A life-sustaining substance is drained out of me. For lack of a better word I call it love. It must be love. What else could it be? Love, dependency, co-dependancy, devotion, hunger, need. Perhaps I'm too young to know. Perhaps I just mistook pain for love.

I still have work, and over time work seems to fill the void. Although I didn't know it at the time—one never does—Madeline's leaving me is actually a good thing. A dose of much needed medicine, it teaches me to how to avoid pain. A simple conditioning exercise. You don't have to be a hard-hearted son-of-a-bitch, but you do have to avoid pain. Ah pain, not knowing which way to turn!

Over time I am able to transfer the pain, first into drink, eventually to other realms. At work, I rise up through the ranks. Simply put, I'm a good editor, creative and thorough. The networks are wide-open in those days. You have to watch who you talk to, of course. No cracks about the War in Vietnam to the wrong people, and no referring to their drivel as "crap."

• • •

I'm crossing Key Bridge on a motorcycle. Drunk out of my mind with the curb looming up at me. Fifty-five miles per hour, much too fast for the notorious Georgetown on-ramp. I bank to the right, trying to avoid it. My front tire hits the curb and I fly out to the middle of the bridge in a heap of dented metal and broken bones. It's 3:00 a.m. No one around. There I am trying to stand up, staggering over this crumpled mess, so drunk I don't even feel my injuries. Instead of going to the hospital, I push the twisted wreck all the way home, smoke a joint and collapse in bed. The next day I go to George Washington Hospital to get patched up.

My father comes down to DC and drives me to High Watch Farm, a facility for recovering alcoholics. I know about AA. My father was one of the pioneers. He ran the farm for many years. I tell him I'm not an alcoholic.

"Okay, you're not an alcoholic. So what's this all about?" he asks.

I start to stammer, then quickly see the uselessness of trying to explain. I don't tell him that Madeleine has run off to Mexico with one of my friends. I can't go off the deep end about my personal love/pain. In my family, you don't make excuses, especially ones grounded in emotional weakness. If I told my father I'd crashed my motorcycle in the middle of Key Bridge at three a.m. on account my girlfriend running off with another guy, he would have told me that you don't mix alcohol and motorcycles. He certainly wouldn't have shown me any pity. I don't deserve any. Deep inside I feel the same way about self-pity. The way it eats into you, causes you to blame others.

"You always liked the Farm," he says. "You can think it over here."

As a boy, I spent a lot of time at High Watch Farm. I understood the AA philosophy and program. In fact, I completely agreed with it. I just didn't think it would ever apply to me. For that matter, neither would psychology. I was an *Übermensch*, serenely capable of finding my own way.

Sure, I know the first thing an alcoholic has to do is stand up and admit he has a problem. When I tell my story, most of them can't believe it.

"Your story is really heavy," says one friend while we're walking in the woods the next day. "And you're only a kid."

"That may be, but I'm not an alcoholic. I don't crave alcohol like you do. If I offered you a drink, put it right in front of you, you couldn't resist."

"AA isn't only about booze, you know," says a female friend.

"So I get drunk from time to time, but I don't wake up desperate for a drink, don't hide liquor under the porch like you."

"Can't you just say you have a problem? Maybe talk to a psychologist?"

"If nothing else, it'll make you feel better."

"I may be fucked up, but I'll work it out," I say. "You know, out here, watching this brook run down the mountain, I'm at peace with the world."

I fish a joint out of my dungaree jacket. My two friends nearly collapse. "How about it?" I ask. "Want to get down?"

6—Intuition

I was filled with remorse for the evil I had done. My longing
for the teaching so obsessed me that I forgot to eat. If I went out, I
wanted to stay in. If I stayed in, I wanted to go out. At night sleep
escaped me. I asked myself unceasingly and passionately by what
means I might practice the true teaching.[12]

> ~ *The Life of Milarepa*—Translated by Lobsang P.
> Lhalungpa

My father tries to get me to stay in New York. A week later, however, I slip back to DC. To the dismay of my co-workers at the network, I quit my job and set myself up as an independent editor. Holding a union card is a prerequisite for most network jobs, and the cards are hard to come by. Everyone thinks my venture will fail. But business is about risk and timing and I've chosen the right moment to go out on my own. Government agencies are gearing up production, embassies want films promoting travel to their countries, and candidates need TV spots for the spectacular 1968 elections. During the campaign, I find myself cutting spots for both parties at the same time. My cottage-industry editing business flourishes. For once, my life seems balanced. Perhaps it's my new girlfriend, Margo. I can't keep up with all the different things she's into. She makes my forays into literature, acting and film appear puny by comparison.

Her attitude is contagious. We carom from one thing to another. I get into Yoga the same way I take up Chinese cooking. Walking through Chinatown one day with Margo, I pick up a cookbook in a variety store. Soon I am tossing vegetables around in a wok. Margo and I become vegetarians. She's researched it, says it's cruel to slaughter dumb animals. I tell her animals aren't dumb. In fact, I once bonded with a cat during an acid trip. Perhaps it's the food, perhaps it's the times, but a short while later, I pick up a book on Hatha Yoga.

We spend a lot of time learning the poses and practicing them. It gets so it doesn't feel right unless we start the day with Yoga. At no time, however, do Margo and I discuss its spiritual aspects. The pure physicality preoccupies us. Years before the appearance of the Yoga mat, Margo sews together some padded quilting to cushion our bodies against the hardwood floors. We lie on our 'mats,' watching and learning from each other, until our movements are synchronized. Sometimes, Yoga practice leads to sex. It seems like a natural extension. Frequently, I am stoned during practice. To me, there is no separation. If I think about the spiritual aspect of my life, it is from the Timothy Leary point of view. According to him, the sacred mushrooms, Yoga, mescaline, pot, Buddhism and LSD share a spiritual connection. I accept the notion that certain drugs stimulate clarity; it happened to me. Once with the cat, once in the GWU Hospital, once on acid in the mountains of West Virginia, lying under a tree with Margo, Roper and friends. Looking up at leaves swaying in the breeze, the flora and fauna come alive. I find myself observing the cellular structure of nature. Or so it seems. I don't realize until much later that I am not even scratching the surface. At the time, however, it's all very meaningful. In my wayward fashion, I'm looking for empirical knowledge. And to be honest, drugs are an instrument, because they lead me back to music.

For me, music is be-bop: Charlie Parker and Miles Davis. As a sixteen-year-old during school vacations, I'd faked my way into the New York jazz clubs: Café Bohemia, Basin Street, Birdland. Even in the Marine Corps where top 40s hits blasted over barracks' AM radios, the black guys knew about Charlie Parker, Dexter Gordon and Clifford Brown.

But in the late 60s jazz changes. Many of my friends believe that musicians like John Coltrane, Albert Ayler, Ornette Coleman, Cecil Taylor and Pharaoh Sanders are spearheading a worldwide spiritual revival. The whole culture is alive with a spiritual buzz, and music is a big part of it. Perhaps, it's mass hypnosis, but like many others, I believe that music will heal the world. It's a small jump from listening to Trane to buying an old saxophone.

I find myself surrounded by a group of black friends playing free jazz music. Margo, who studied classical piano, jumps into it with me. We practice a lot, devoting our time to music and Yoga. Most of the musicians I play with are former bop players who want to learn to play *free*. They appreciate our Columbia Road apartment located over a bank. There's no one in the building after work hours, so we can go all night. The more I play *with* them, the more I want to play *like* them; to master the be-bop changes—scales, chords, harmonies.

From my present perspective, it's unclear what I was thinking at a time when people were looking everywhere for spiritual meaning. While some people play Beatles recordings backwards in search of spiritual truth, my friends and I listen to John Coltrane and Sun Ra. Spiritual meaning is believed to be just within reach, if only you listen to the right music, eat the right food and smoke the right dope. What is meaningful for me is the effort I put into the instrument. Once again, of course, I fail. This time, however, failure leads to the root of my imperfection. I begin to realize that the problem is not my inability to excel—at math, at writing, at acting, at filmmaking, or at music. The problem is why. *Why can't I excel at anything? What happened to make failure inevitable?*

Sensing my frustration, Margo proposes a trip to Europe. She gives our stuff away. In typical fashion, she just wants to go, not waste a lot of time bartering or arranging for storage. No time for me to change my mind. Hey, I'm eager to go, too. But it's hard to part with my books and records. I sulk a bit, but by then everything's packed, sold or promised. I don't know what to expect, but I do sense a change of perspective is the key to overcoming my self-destructive tendencies.

● ● ●

Before leaving, my father invites us to his home in Kent, Connecticut for a pow-wow where he presents me with a book "The Master Game," spiritual reading matter by a guy named DeRopp. In it he inscribes:

> Welcome, O life! I go to encounter for the millionth time the reality of experience and to forge in the smithy of my soul the uncreated conscience of my race.
>
> ~ *A Portrait of an Artist as a Young Man*—James Joyce

I look at my father. Nothing on his face betrays the reasons behind the inscription. It's probably the most-unexpected and the most-welcome gift of my life.

It's as if he's resigned from the parent role. It has obviously failed and made us both miserable. Now he's reinventing himself as an older acquaintance, someone I might actually be able to communicate with. And while it pleases me, it also surprises me.

Then I remember: AA. My father's involvement with Bill Wilson during the early days of AA. He learned the ropes from *The Master*. And what is more spiritual in this consumer society than

Alcoholics Anonymous with its reliance on a higher power to over-come alcoholic addiction?

I'm about twelve the first time I attend an AA meeting where my father is the featured speaker. I remember the force of his oratory, how he stood back from life, an ironic observer who used humor to engage his audience, then tragedy and tenderness to move them.

How little I know about him!

Not that I should know; every man's life is private and my father was under no obligation to share his. After all, we have shut each other out to the point of estrangement. Now the only one who might make an overture has done so. It gets me to thinking. What do I really know about my father?

When I was a rugrat, perhaps he changed my diapers, took me to the park.

But the only real foray I can remember was a trip to the Polo Grounds to see Willie Mays and Bobby Thomson. And I had to coax him into that.

Maybe he cared but never found a way to show it. Maybe I'm to blame. I could see myself as a young jerk, unable to understand where he was coming from.

Perhaps he only feels comfortable letting me into his outer world of golf and tennis. His inner world—the place where he comes face-to-face with his demons—well, that's personal. Maybe he thinks I won't understand.

But if he didn't think I could understand, why did he encourage me to attend so many AA meetings? Naw, he really ignored me most of my life.

Which leads me to something my mother told me: as soon as my father quit drinking, he stopped being a warm human being. But how much of it was just my mother's bias? Surely not her story about the cops calling up to tell her they found him passed out and beaten up in the gutter along 3rd Avenue with a three-year-old boy standing over him tugging at his arm. After that incident, my mother didn't let me out with my father again, not until after the war when he sobered up and joined AA.

All through childhood I try to recall the incident from memory, but can't—so I recreate it in my mind a thousand times.

Dressed in my Eton jacket and shorts, I picture myself and my father setting out, and my mother waving and smiling, sensing impending disaster, powerless to prevent it. Proudly, I walk down the summer New York streets alongside my father. I imagine all sorts of pleasures: amusement rides, parks and swings, cotton candy—before ending up on 3rd Avenue with the El vibrating the street below. My father picks me up and points as the roaring trains go by.

At first, the bar is not so bad. Laughter and activity, the won-der-world of adults at play. *So this is what they do.* Tall stools, and sawdust on the floor to play with. The fight breaks out. The noise, the confusion, my father on the floor, lying in the sawdust. The smell of overturned whiskey covering us. The heave-ho, and I'm standing in the receding daylight, crying and pulling on my father's arm when the police arrive.

I run the high points of my father's life. A long bender during the Depression, right up to the middle of the War. Then, in late '43, the US Army. Still a drunk, he has a hard time, but by the time the War ends, he's come to accept the necessity of sobering up. He finds Bill Wilson and AA, and never takes another drink. I marvel at his determination and swear someday, now that my mother has passed, to ask him about the day we ended up in the gutter.

• • •

After six months of backpacking through France, Italy, Greece and Spain, we're finishing our trip in a Moroccan hotel. Margo wants to make a beeline for home.

"I'm not ready," I tell her. "Let's go back to Paris."

"Thinking about the jazz scene?" she asks.

"Naw, I'm just not ready to go back."

I'm almost finished packing, only a few items left to stash when Margo starts to bug me about paying the bill.

"You won't stop until I go downstairs and pay."

"Go downstairs; I'll take care of everything," she says.

When I come back, I find Margo standing on a chair by the window, cutting the curtains down with a large pair of scissors.

"What the hell are you doing?" I ask.

"I like this material," she says.

"What are you going to do with it? It's faded." I'm dumb-founded. I can think of a lot of things to do in this hotel room, but cutting down the curtains isn't one of them.

"I'm going to make a dress," says Margo.

"We can find something better in the Medina."

"I like this pattern."

"Well, let's get out of here before they put us in a Moroccan prison."

"Relax."

As if I could relax. Suddenly, every sound on the stairs is the manager or the cleaning lady or the cops.

"Will you hurry up!"

"Go over to the café and order breakfast if you're so nervous."

"I'm not leaving here without you. Where are you going to put…" I walk over to the curtains. "God, they're mangy. And you don't have any room in your pack."

"Stop worrying. You paid the bill, didn't you?"

"I didn't pay for a lot of moth-eaten curtains."

"Go over to the café, will you?"

"I won't leave without you. This is insane."

We walk through the lobby, not the slightest trace of guilt on Margo's face. I'm beet red and at a loss. Finding the recent National Teacher Award candidate standing on a chair in a Tangiers hotel room cutting down the curtains doesn't make sense.

We sit in the café eating breakfast. It's right across the little square from the hotel. From where we're sitting I can see the window of our room, and all the other rooms, for that matter. Ours is the only one without curtains, and I pray they are safely tucked away in Margo's backpack with no telltale remnants hanging out. I look down at her pack.

"Stop worrying," she insists.

"I can't."

All through breakfast, through every bite of my Moroccan croissant, I can't take my eye off that hotel window. Margo has no such problem. She holds forth on Paris and the jazzy life people lead there.

"Pretty soon, you'll be sitting in with Stan Getz," she says.

"Margo, do we have to discuss this now? Let's get out of here."

Margo gets up and walks to the counter where she buys the *International Herald Tribune* for the boat trip. When I glance back at the hotel window, there's a woman—the maid, I think—waving at us. She's screaming in Arabic through the curtain-less window. I imagine what she's saying: *Son of a goat, come back, you thief. I will have you boiled in olive oil along with the rest of the scurvy infidels who have invaded our peaceful country with your guidebooks, backpacks and short-shorts.*

Margo waves back and smiles. Hastily, I stand up and throw down some money, more than enough for the note. I wave off the woman and drag Margo up by the arm, a half-eaten croissant dangling from her mouth.

"Let's go."

Reluctantly, Margo stands up, hoists her pack, and waves at the window. "*L'hôtel était merveilleux,*" she shouts.

"*Merci,*" I cry, almost in tears.

Looking back over my shoulder as we push through the crowded streets, I'm almost flogging her to keep the pace.

The next morning on the boat, Margo unpacks the curtains and spreads them out on the bunk. Dusty, dirty, raggedy, there they lie. I open my pack to look for my rose-colored bellbottoms.

"Where are my pants?" I ask.

Margo shrugs and begins to turn red.

"Margo, they were on the bed when I went down to pay the bill. Now where are they?"

They're my favorite pants, the perfect symbol of the sixties, purchased at Bloomingdale's on the way out of New York.

After a moment, it hits me. The maid. That's what she was screaming about—my pants. But I couldn't go back because Margo had cut down the stupid curtains. The maid was waving at us to come back for the pants. That's what she was holding and screaming about; she didn't give a shit about the curtains, hadn't even noticed they were missing.

The perfect absurdity makes it bearable, but the pants become an obstacle between us. Margo's object lesson has backfired and now she feels guilty, at least until I tell her my reason for leaving the café in such a hurry.

"See," says Margo, "you were worried about nothing. We could have gone back and you'd have your pants."

"Why are you saying this to me?" I ask. "Under the circumstances, I couldn't go back there any more than I could eat a tarantula. I had a lump of hash on me the size of the Hope Diamond and I wasn't going back no how, no way…even if I hadn't been holding."

"You had a lump of hash? You have it now?"

"Yes, yes, yes."

"And you intend to go through customs in Naples off a boat from Morocco with a lump of hash the size of a tarantula?"

"I don't know…I thought I'd smoke it and then give the rest to one of the weirdoes on this ship. The mad-dog Englishman, the one who walked across the Kalahari Desert, or the guy with the mixed-blood wife, you know, the South African couple."

"Give me that hash right now. I'm throwing it overboard."

"I will not; it's a long voyage."

"Then promise me," she begs, "that what you and your weird friends don't smoke on the trip, you'll throw away before we land."

•   •   •

For a finale to our trip, Margo suggests visiting the shrine of the Sibyl at Cumae, the precursor to the modern city of Naples. I hate touristy attractions, hate mingling with people in museums and buses. But for some reason, the idea grabs me. All of a sudden, I have to see the Oracle. I don't know why. Normally, I resist feel-good vibes and presentiments, but I want to see the Cumaean Sibyl.

When we get to the site, I go off by myself, sit down near the cave of the Oracle and ask myself out loud, "What am I supposed to do? Where am I supposed to go?"

No one around. No tourists, nobody. Margo has drifted away, exploring other parts of the site. Suddenly, the answer appears. Not in the form of words. I find myself flying over Paris, as if on a morphine booster only I'm clean. I fly over Notre Dame, *le Grand Palais*, the Louvre, along the Seine. *Go to Paris,* says a voice. *Alone.*

Now, that's the kind of sign I like, straightforward and unambiguous. Don't know where it came from, some form of autosuggestion, my conversation with Margo, catching Stan Getz at the *Chat Qui Pêche* when we passed through Paris...whatever.

The next morning, I tell Margo I'm going to explore the expatriate jazz scene in Paris. From the querulous expression on her face, I realize she thinks I've had my mind made up all along. Then I tell her the real reason.

"The Cumaean Sybil told me."

"What?"

"I had a kind of auto-séance. The Sybil told me to go."

"What are you saying? That you had a vision?"

"Not a real vision, not like the Lady of Lourdes," I say. "Margo, I have a problem. I keep it hidden because I'm not sure what it's all about, like a recurring dream."

"What dream?"

"Something to do with an accident as a kid."

"What happened?"

"I don't remember much...only I'm convinced I'll find the answer in Paris."

It's one of those rare moments of truth in a lifetime. A decision based on pure intuition, which, unfortunately, doesn't leave Margo much room to maneuver. She decides to go home. I tell her I have no idea how long my expedition will last.

"In that case," she says, "let's not put limits on each other."

"As far as other people, you mean?"

She nods, looks down at her feet. It's our way of condoning sex with other partners during our separation—without mentioning the word. By the time she raises her eyes, I feel her relief, as if she's realized that people just grow tired of each other and it is, all in all, no big deal. She smiles, and right away I want to take her, but there's a barrier between us now. So I smile back and help her shoulder her pack. Then she turns around and suddenly she's in my arms, and I'm squeezing and kissing her. Teary-eyed and never so fetching, all her Irish charms on display, she tells me we can get back together when I come to my senses.

In Rome, I go to the station to pick up the tickets for Paris. On the way out I meet a girl. During a brief conversation, I tell her I am going to Paris to play the saxophone. She tells me she'll be passing through Paris in three weeks and will write me c/o American Express. Sounds great—summer in Paris, a beautiful girl, a romantic tryst, a fresh start, renewal.

I reach Paris in early August and start looking for a place to live. I find a small apartment on the rue Quincampoix. Only one condition: the present occupants are staying until late September, but as I don't have loads of money, I can't quibble…except that without an apartment I can't practice. The hotel I find in the Latin Quarter is only 18 francs a night. I move in and go looking for a place to practice.

Expatriates I run across tell me about *the* place, The American Center on Bd. Raspail, an immense old building once owned by Chateaubriand. During August, the Center is closed. Most musicians are on tour or vacation. But I've just come off an extended trip. I'm glutted with sun and Retsina wine, eager to get to work. Everyone says I'll have to wait for the *Rentrée*, the moment the French return to Paris. To pass the time I explore the city, making sure to check the mail counter at American Express regularly. Even though we met briefly, a sixth sense tells me that Paulette will show up. But with the city half-empty, my limited routine soon becomes monotonous. I don't know anyone, I have no place to practice, and I am anxious about Paulette. Toward the end of August a letter arrives, and by the end of the week we are living an interlude, which, according to popular song, only happens during *April in Paris*.

In spite of our carnal attraction and the perfect surroundings, Paulette is a practical person. She wants a serious relationship.

"It's a shame you don't have a place to practice. I want to hear you play," she says. "I know you're really good."

"Well," I say, "as soon as the American Center opens."

"That can't happen, baby. I've got to get home by September 15th and I want you to come with me."

I should be flattered by her encouragement, but I have serious doubts about my ability. In DC, amidst a flurry of drugs, drink, and low expectations, I was considered *avant-garde*. Lord knows, I tried hard enough. I practiced dutifully. Perhaps she'll like my playing.

But the problem isn't music; it's convincing Paulette to stay in Paris. I take her to my future apartment, thinking I can pique her interest with visions of a place of our own and a daring expatriate life. After dinner, Paulette picks up Doug's guitar and plays amazing original music for 45 minutes. I didn't know she could play. I am devastated. She is way beyond me. I picture her face after hearing just ten bars. She'll be on the next flight back to New Jersey. Fortunately, I never find a place to play before her scheduled departure.

Before leaving, Paulette tells me she can't live a bohemian life. If I want her, she will wait a short time. Even though Margo and I still plan to get back together, I am tempted. However, something holds me back. Perhaps it's the Cumaean Sibyl.

I picture my failures repeating themselves, Madeleine and Margo all over again. If I hook up with Paulette in New Jersey, my inadequacies will be revealed. I'll wind up commuting to New York to cut film and never find what's wrong with me.

"I'll be back in a year," I say. "First I have to see if I've got what it takes."

"If you can't make up your mind, I don't want to hear from you again," are Paulette's final words.

• • •

Before it is unceremoniously pulled down and replaced by the Cartier Foundation Museum, a modern building of lesser charm, the American Center is the meeting place for artists from all countries and features activities and classes in dance, Yoga, music, theater, Tai Chi and painting. For someone like me, blending in with this assortment of talent and eccentricity isn't much of a challenge. The cracks are large and I fall into one. Namely, the strugglers, those musicians who practice a lot yet make little forward progress: a motley brotherhood with faulty intonation, a shoddy sense of rhythm and poor pitch. There are the true professionals, of course. The Art Ensemble of Chicago, Gato Barbieri, The Black Artists Group, Anthony

Braxton, Steve Lacy, all of whom give eagerly awaited concerts at the Center. I get Steve Lacy's address and call him about lessons.

"Play this note and hold it," he says during my first lesson. I play a C, then a D, then an octave higher. Long notes are all he wants. For an hour, I play while he listens.

"Now vary the intensity without changing the pitch," he instructs.

As I huff and puff, Steve listens. From the frown on his face, I can tell something is wrong.

"You go in and out of pitch." He plays a note on his soprano. "See?" Then he sounds a note on the piano. "Now, sing the note." So I sing. "As the dynamics change, it wanders all over the place, your note does. Your problem isn't musical; there's something wrong with your breathing. I can't help you. It's not related to music. The music just shows it up."

"What can I do?"

"Train yourself to hear what you're doing. And play these," he says, writing down a series of notes in my book. "Practice them until you can control them. Apart from that, there are ways, but you'll have to look outside of music."

I walk home wondering what the hell he is talking about. *Something wrong with my breathing? What, for instance? I'm walking and breathing!* Yet, as disappointed as I am, it's a relief. I have something to go on. I redouble my efforts, practicing the simple exercises for hours. I will master them.

By my next lesson there is no improvement. I can sense Steve's frustration. The same as mine, only more so. *Who wants to work with a guy who isn't even at the starting blocks?* Steve tells me that I have a long way to go. After a few more lessons, I stop going. What's the point? I have to look elsewhere.

I end my relationship with alcohol. Funny how, surrounded by the alcohol that flows so freely in France, I feel no desire to consume it. The image of fumes rising from stale cigarette butts and half-finished drinks in the aftermath of Washington parties revolts me. Slowly, I modulate from lost weekends to an occasional beer or glass of wine. I never think about quitting, the thirst just disappears. Hashish, on the other hand, makes me a better player, or so I think. But surely drinking has been part of my problem. Perhaps quitting will help my breathing.

I stay up in my top floor apartment for hours, playing along with records, blasting away at the saxophone. Yet, when I frequent the practice rooms in the basement of the Center and ask to play with other musicians, I am shunned. Down in the basement of the Center, what the French refer to as *la Cave*, are four or five first-come-first-served practice rooms. Down there, amid the all-pervading smell of cannabis, they want no part of me. Sure, they're polite—but firm. We can joke together and hang out, but playing together is another thing. This isn't like Washington; this is serious. Musicians trying to make a living, competing for the few available gigs. It isn't garage-style jazz.

Through an acquaintance, I'm invited to meet Gato Barbieri and though my friend says the occasion is banal, it turns out to be anything but. Gato has been invited to try out a new Selmer saxophone at their showroom and we are invited to be present. The acquaintance doesn't show up, but I do. It's Gato, his wife, Michelle, and me. Gato is ushered into a small, soundproofed room by a fawning suit carrying a shiny new Selmer tenor on a velvet cloth. The suit lingers for a moment while Gato fingers the sax. All the while I'm thinking: this is the first time I've been inches away from a professional musician. Sure the guys I've played with had their own sound, and it was cool. So, I'm thinking he'll sound pretty much like every other musician.

Then he puts the mouthpiece to his lips and the room seems to expand. The power of his sound literally blows the walls down. I look at Michelle. She's watching Gato and smiling. The suit ducks out of the room after a moment while Gato continues blowing for fifteen minutes. I can feel the power, the purity of every note, the mastery of every slight degree of pitch and intensity...the range, the harmonics, the growls. Suddenly, I think about a boy. And I realize that I once possessed such purity—and somehow, I lost it. I leave the showroom with feelings of euphoria and gloom. Euphoria because of the beauty and power of Gato's playing; gloom because I finally understand what Steve Lacy has been telling me: my problem is not musical. Gato's playing illustrates it clearly.

Labeled as a struggler, I persist, practicing every day. The more I think about Steve Lacy's words, the more I realize I must understand the root cause. But how? I redouble my Yoga practice and begin to look for books on breathing. That's how I meet Michelle Rubin, browsing through the esoteric books at Galignani's. She's at the same bin and asks me what I am looking for.

"I'm not really sure. A book on breath control, I guess."

I try my expatriate musician line. It works well enough to get her back to my apartment where she forthrightly refuses to sleep with me. I ask her why. She laughs and tells me that she is in no shape for sex; she's into macrobiotics in a big way. And adds that, even if she were up for sex, she wouldn't, not with me. Then she asks me to play the saxophone.

"I want to hear you."

Nervously, I attach the mouthpiece to my sax and start blowing. When I'm finished, she tells me my body is the problem.

"What do you mean?" I ask.

"Take off your shirt," she commands.

I try joking: "Only if you take yours off."

"I'm serious. Take off your shirt."

I take my shirt off. "Look at yourself," she says, "Your abdomen. You can't get enough air."

"I can't?"

"Breathe in."

For twenty minutes, she watches me breathe in and out, feeling my abdomen as I inhale and exhale.

"There's no abdominal action; it's all superficial breathing."

A few days later, she comes back to tell me she's returning to the States. The macrobiotic diet is killing her. I don't understand, but am curious to learn why she's come back. She isn't interested in me, not sexually, but here she is, lecturing me on breathing and macrobiotics. Where has she come from, this creature who's gotten me to take off my shirt?

I am expecting her to leave me with a few final words of wisdom when she stands up to retrieve her bag, pulling out a book with a yellow dust cover.

"This book will help your breathing. In fact, it will change your life."

"How?"

"Why do you think we met?"

"You fell for my line?"

"So you could get this book. It contains the secret of life, you know."

Then she nibbles me on the cheek and leaves. I never see her again.

• • •

A few days later, I'm at Galignani's, standing by the same bin. I look down at the books. Two copies of the *The Secret of the Golden Flower* lie tucked among the many volumes. Just then, I feel the spirit of Michelle Rubin flood over me—the living embodiment of the Cumaean Sybil. If I hadn't met her, I would never have picked up that particular book. The mystical drawing on the bright yellow jacket, the Chinese characters—not the type of book I had in mind. According to Michelle Rubin, it contains the secret of life. *That's just dandy. It'll probably remain a secret, because I don't understand a bloody word.* I do realize it's a kind meditation, but an ancient text like this? I certainly didn't think it had anything to do with breathing.

So I try Zen meditation in the 14th Arrondissement. The well-known Japanese Zen Master talks all the time while everyone hums. I get bored. Not bored, I just don't understand what's supposed to happen. What am I supposed to feel? Whatever it is, I'm not able to connect.

The Secret of the Golden Flower, on the other hand, is written in a kind of poetic style, which, though hard to understand, challenges me in a literary sense. I feel a renewed interest in poetry, like my first encounter with ee cummings or Hopkins. It's not like I sit down and read it cover to cover. I don't. It's not a narrative kind of book. It's a manual, albeit an ancient one. At first, I forget all about it. I spend months chasing women and exploring the Parisian demimonde. In fits and starts, a year goes by. Finally one morning after my Yoga practice, I sit down, my legs crossed in the lotus position.

7—Renunciation

The Primal Spirit loves stillness, and the Conscious Spirit loves movement. In its movement it remains bound to feelings and desires. Day and night it wastes the primal seed till the energy of the Primal Spirit is entirely used up. Then the Conscious Spirit leaves the shell and goes away.[13]

> ~ *The Secret of the Golden Flower*—Lu Yen - Richard Wilhelm, Translator

For some reason, this time meditation is real. Not that it jumps all the way to the front burner, it doesn't. There are so many other things going on. At first, there's a lot of thrashing around, trying to get comfortable in the lotus position. Everything in *The Secret of the Golden Flower* is expressed in an esoteric fashion, for example: "Anyone can talk about reflection, but he cannot master it if he does not know what the word means. What has to be reversed by reflection is the self-conscious heart, which has to direct itself toward that point where the formative spirit is not yet manifest."[14]

What the hell does it mean? I sort of know; I sort of don't. If it's mere poetry, I'm wasting my time looking for hidden meaning. If it's a roadmap, will it lead somewhere, that is, once I decipher it? Yet something tells me it *is* the real thing—an arcane text bursting at the seams with the mysteries and secrets most people don't value until life gets really ugly.

In three months, I advance as far as Section 3, *The Circulation of the Light and the Protection of the Center*, where it is written: "Only when the eyelids are lowered properly halfway is the tip of the nose seen in just the right way. Therefore it is taken as a guide-line...so that the eyes are brought into the right direction for looking, and then are held to the guide-line: after that one can let it be. That is the way a mason hangs a plumb-line. As soon as he has hung it up, he guides his work by it without continually bothering himself to look at the plumb-line."[15]

If the 'formative spirit is not yet manifest,' at least I understand the notion of the plumb-line, a sort of 'inner gyroscope,' a way of 'centering oneself' in order to tune out extraneous detail. I imagine months of boring effort in the lotus position, troubled by thoughts that stretch back to childhood and are impossible to control. *What does the formative spirit look like? Will I recognize it, if and when it ever appears?*

I learn to sit with my attention fixed on the tip of my nose—and not much else. Most of the time I notice no difference. Besides observing my nose, I am supposed to regulate my breathing, but because nothing happens, I constantly wonder if I am doing it correctly. Only when I am walking, which in Paris is often and far, am I able to follow my breath unperturbed, that is, to force exhalation and inhalation into a rhythmic cycle. I time the length of a single breath over a given number of strides. Inhale four counts or strides, hold four, exhale four, hold four, start over. Over countless kilometers of Parisian streets I observe the source of my breathing as it descends lower and lower, and I begin to visualize my abdomen as a pump. With my attention fixed on my breathing, I notice that my thoughts wander less and my mind is still.

I put my horn away. Walking, meditating and practicing Yoga is all I do for the next six months. Then one day on one of my walks I find myself in front of the American Center with my saxophone. I go straight into the basement, prepare the horn and stick the reed to my lips. What comes out surprises me. I am playing—not like before when I easily ran out of breath, or when two successive tones refused to respect proper intonation, or when a single tone sounded slightly different each time. I am in the basement of the American Center, and in spite of the three-year-old reed, what issues forth is clear, distinct and powerful. After a moment I stop, trying to contain my wonderment at what is happening. It's not Gato, but it's surprisingly good.

I feel the registers of the saxophone resonate in different parts of my body. The high notes feel as if they are coming off the top of my head, the low ones—the lower the note, the more profound the feeling—feel like they are coming out of my loins, sometimes from the soles of my feet. It's as if I only need to direct my breath up and down from head to toe—and the instrument plays itself.

I play some more. No recognizable tune, just a flurry of notes from the top to the bottom registers of the horn. Musicians, used to all the regulars, peek into my room. Some are shocked to see me (they've heard me struggle for so long). Sunny Murray pops his head in, raises his thumbs, and tells me to keep it up. Several others, who formerly spurned me, now invite me to play. Politely I tell them, "No." I don't feel ready. Or rather, I haven't finished. That's it. I am in the midst of something, not at the end. My horn is merely a monitoring device for the profound changes my body is undergoing. The tones I produce are like the waveform of an oscilloscope. If the tones and intonation are pure, I am making progress meditating.

Something transformational is going on. It isn't *mental*; it's *physical*. It exists in me. Experiential—a word I wouldn't have used six months ago. It's the result of my homemade breathing exercises, almost as if I have discovered a secret control knob and turned it just a teeny-weeny bit. Perhaps this back and forth between meditation and music can be sustained. Perhaps I have something to be serious about, to excel at, even.

During my next meditation, my attention is loose and scattered. Perhaps I am overeager, expecting too much. I lose track of the breath count. I am too stirred up by what happened at the Center, already seduced by fame and fortune. I have found the magic key and now visualize my name in lights. Okay, just a modest fame; I'm not greedy, but my mind is out of control. My former life is staging a comeback. It views this music revival as the perfect pretext to reassume control. *How willful the mind! The slightest crack, the slightest opening, it slips its tether like a mad dog. It lets you drink from a cup of power you don't possess, lets you build a name on credit. Whereas I should be walking and counting my breath.*

Why does walking produce results? Could it be because I am not distracted? Or am I not following the method? Am I somehow off the path, headed for derailment? The book talks about that, too. "The ensnaring world is where the five kinds of dark demons disport themselves. This is the case, for example, when, after fixation, one has chiefly thoughts of dry wood and dead ashes, and few thoughts of the bright spring on the great earth. In this way, one sinks into the world of the dark. If one tarries there long, one enters the world of plants and stones."[16] I don't want to end up a stone.

• • •

One night late in the American Center, I play until I am standing apart from myself, watching the horn-player, *me*, from the other side of a mirror. Jean-Pierre, a French alto player, comes by to listen as I run some scales. He offers me a joint. I refuse. We play for the next two hours, first in the basement, then upstairs on the stage. It's a quiet night, no concerts or *spectacles*, as the French call them. Just two musicians. We attract a large audience. I am all over the horn from growls to harmonics, something that I have never been able to do. All I do is exhale and the flow of air to the reed does the rest. As long as I have air, the fingerings don't matter. Zoning, someone calls it. I am in a zone, says the audience. By about 11:00 p.m. we kind of peter out, and I pack up and leave the Center.

Another wet Paris night. I forge ahead into the drizzle hardly able to keep from falling or bumping into things. I lurch through the streets seeking the magic rabbit hole up and out of *Wonderland* and back to the side of the mirror known as *Reality*. But something is holding me in thrall. An energy coursing through me, almost blinding me. The street signs, the buildings, the metro stations—while all familiar—are unreal. One big blurry panorama—as if I am inside an Impressionist painting, a nightscape on the Quai de la Tournelle, a Seurat or a Monet.

I see double. The explosion of energy has tinted my eyeballs such that everything appears a kind of dull gray. I am dumbstruck and dazed. A madman, going madder in a hurry. Vaguely, I start for a friend's on the rue de Vaugirard, but never get there. I lose track of where I am going. In fact, I don't have a destination. Worse, the whole notion of destination suddenly evaporates, and I am just staggering, content to be lunging forward, counting. One, two, three, four. The world in 4/4 time. I bump into a lamppost and excuse myself. I am not drunk, lost or mad. I am tired, yet can't sleep; I am exhausted, yet just keep counting over and over.

How long am I out there? I don't know; all I know is I never get to my friend's house. In fact, I have no recollection of how far I walk, where I go, or what I see. It's what sees me that worries me. What disembodied creatures are sustaining me, preventing me from staggering into the Seine, my horn case floating up next to lovers under a willow tree? What audience of invisible *voyeurs* watches my slightly listing body crash headlong into the rain? I wander around Paris in the drizzle listening to a strange, unearthly music in my head.

The constant rush of energy surges from below, coursing through my brain, pushing my eyes out of their sockets. It is so fierce and so relentless that it clogs all remnants of spatial awareness. All night I stagger around with blurred, double vision, mumbling streams of disassociated free verse until, finally, I realize it is the meditation beckoning me, wrapping itself around me, pulling me under its sway.

Somehow, throughout the night, I remain ambulatory, in a trance perhaps, but upright. The Michelin Man floating through Paris, bumping into lampposts, trying to shake double vision and a throbbing pulse in his head. The next thing I know it is morning and I am sitting at the *Petit Bar* with a Spanish chick who is trying to convince me to go to Alsace to work the *vendange*.

Sometimes I have to walk for hours just to be able to sleep. That is the end of drugs. I haven't used them for a while now; I flush the rest away. No booze; I haven't tasted a drop for over a year. With all this excess energy flowing through me, I don't need outside stimuli. At the same time I feel weak, the need to rest. But isn't that what metamorphosis is all about?

More than once, it occurs to me that, yes, I should be doing this under the guidance of a 'teacher.' But where to find one? If I can't find one, I have to go on alone. I have no choice. It isn't like I can choose my *Enlightenment Dream Team* and go off to mini-camp for spiritual calisthenics. Sure, there are warnings. So-called enlightened friends simply say: Don't look for a teacher; your teacher will find you. Somewhere, sometime, somehow, some place. But what if my teacher has already found me?—in the form of a book. One given to me by a girl, a total stranger, a living embodiment of the Cumaean Sybil. A book I put away for nearly a year and almost threw away. A book I eventually come back to, stay with, and ultimately begin to decipher. *What if this is my Way, my Tao?*

• • •

The longer I stay in Paris, the more involved I become. The women seem to be flowing as freely as the wine and the hash. I have a theory that they are attracted to my madness. I no longer need drugs or wine, for I am in the center of a whirlwind. Everything opens up for me. But as more and more enticements surround me, beckoning me not to take my practice seriously, I sense danger. I can't give up meditating—not now, not when something's finally happening. I must suppress all external influences.

> "That is what the Master means when he says that every
> entanglement in thought of other people and oneself must
> be completely given up.[17]"

The Yin and Yang of life is amazing. I am into a practice that is changing my being. At the same time I am tempted. I try to think of a place in the US where can I get away from TV and Richard Nixon, the Black Panthers and the Weathermen, *The Young and the Restless*, my father and all the other people I know. I'd need $20,000, and I still might wind up in a desert camp run by Manson-style maniacs. No, I have to stay in France. No one knows me and I won't get ensnarled in outside events because I don't follow them. I barely know the name of the French Prime Minister. And all I know about French politics is that they have a Communist Party, which seems more conventional than the American Republican Party.

I have money from my film editing work. The only question is where to go. I stash my sax on the rue de Vaugirard. My head is exploding, energy still coursing through it. I start to walk. When I get to my destination, the *Café des Deux Saules*, I order an *Omelette Parmentière* and try to think.

I don't need to do much thinking. Seated at the next table is Isabelle, my ex-landlord. She waves to me and I change tables. The guy with her is Hungarian, a painter. Isabelle tells me about a house in the village of St. Jean de la Blaquière, down the mountain from her house in St. Privat. She is the exclusive rental agent for the American girl from Chicago, who owns this huge house in the center of town, pop. 328. The house rents for 200 francs a month, about $40. The house, she says, has fifteen rooms, but only the main room, a quasi-bedroom, and a kind of primitive bathroom, are inhabitable. There is gas and electricity, but no hot water.

"That's why it's so cheap, *chéri*," she says.

"So if I rent it for a year," I ask, "no one is going to show up?"

"If you live there, it will be like erasing your name from the registers of humanity. You can send the money directly to Sarah in Chicago. No one would rent it otherwise; it's not really livable."

•   •   •

Had I spoken to any knowledgeable person about my meditation, they would have told me, if not killing myself, at the very least I was going about it the wrong way. I wonder if having to walk for hours to regulate my breathing, blurred vision and hallucinations, and the sudden ability to play music are a test to see if I have what it takes to get to the next level, but there is no one to ask. And that's what saves me. I have to start trusting my body. For I am still far from my perfect body, and radical action without regard to conventional wisdom is the only way of getting back to it. Medically it sounds counter-intuitive, but I know I'm right. *I must go back to the moment before my conception. And I believe that I have found the one method of doing it.*

But if it's just a question of strengthening body tissue and muscle structure, why not bodybuilding? Well, before leaving DC I tried working out in a gym. But the splinter has torqued my body out of alignment, making the left side of my back stronger than the right, and the right side of my front (the opposite side) stronger than the left. And instead of equally balancing my frame all around, lifting weights only exacerbated my torqued condition. Seen from above, my shoulders are like a skewed figure eight. You know, the way teachers explain a parallelogram to their students, as *a rectangle that some one sat on.* Well, my torso is like a figure eight that someone has sat on. How did it happen? Quite simply, I imploded as the splinter blocked off nerve conduits to parts of my body, thereby denying those parts vital growth energy. Quite understandable, if you're living it. If you're not, I wonder. Does anyone understand? It's a process similar to the way a damaged tree limb withers when, for one reason or another, its vital growth energy is choked off.

Moreover, as I eventually find out, meditation is more powerful than bodybuilding. Meditation works from the inside-out; bodybuilding works from the outside-in. It supplies no vital growth energy. In fact, it uses it up. The more I lifted weights, the more I reinforced my deformity. The more force I applied, the more deformed I became. No, I have to finesse my body and neither bodybuilding nor any other method, including Yoga, will work. Only the restorative meditation I practice can rewind my being backwards to the moment of the splinter, and then run it forward again. To reunite with my perfect body I have to reopen the nerve conduits that were blocked off. And that means absolute stillness of the kind meditation requires.

Early in *The Secret of the Golden Flower*, on the first page in fact, lies this innocent phrase: *action in order to attain non-action*. I've passed over it many times without realizing what it means. This deceptively simple phrase is the root purpose of meditation, the most powerful principle in the universe. Supreme power is stillness; stillness is supreme power.

> The great One is the term given to that which has nothing above it. The secret of the magic of life consists in using action to attain non-action. One must not wish to leap over everything and penetrate directly.[18]

8—Discovery

In the case of those in whom the awakening occurs all at once as a result of Yoga or other spiritual practices, the sudden impact of powerful vital currents on the brain and other organs is often attended with grave risk and strange mental conditions, varying from moment to moment, exhibiting in the beginning, the abnormal peculiarities of a medium, mystic, genius, and madman all rolled into one.[19]

~ *Kundalini: The Evolutionary Energy in Man*—Gopi Krishna

My first night in St. Jean is spent trying to stay warm. There are 15 rooms on three unheated floors, unlived in for three years. I move my suitcase of clothes and duffel bag of books and records into the bedroom.

I am too weak to continue playing, so I put my saxophone away, wondering if my sudden ability was only a dream. With my body changing almost daily, will I ever get back to music? Or was music merely a prelude to something bigger?

I can no longer live with people. No one understands this, least of all my family. They prescribe doctors and treatments, a job, and a dose of growing up and facing responsibility. And they have every reason to see things that way. I have no track record, not in music, acting, or writing, in fact, not in human relations. I even gave up film editing just as it was becoming gainful. That, of course, bewilders my family. They pile on my father, who in turn simply throws up his arms and exclaims that he hasn't heard from me.

Even though I think about playing music and about friends, I don't want to be anywhere else. Paris, sure, I think about it. The wild six months before coming down south. But I see it as a final temptation, a holding out to me of all life's creature comforts.

My broken-down house, the den-like bedroom, the large room and walk-in fireplace, which exists at the exact center of the house, is like the center of my being. The rooms pre-exist (if such a word can be used) only as vague outlines of what they once were, much like the undeveloped nature of my true being.

The fireplace is the belly of the house and produces the energy that holds it upright. I can stand in it. My first purchase is a truck-load of wood. Only when the fireplace is functioning is the large room inhabitable. If I do not have wood, I will have to retreat into the bedroom with its expensive electric heater. I must secure the limits of my world. I must be able to inhabit the large room. During the day the room is warm enough, but at night, even with sweaters piled on, the dampness makes it too uncomfortable to sit and read. The fortress thick walls keep the extreme cold out, but over time the damp works its way in.

The kitchen's in the corner next to the fireplace. Scattered old sofas and chairs whose dust billows in a cloud when I sit, the large windows facing the narrow street, are part of the 2nd Empire charm, but the fireplace holds the key to the house.

On the phone to the mill, I discuss wood and price, but the owner keeps using an expression I don't understand. I keep asking him to explain. He keeps repeating that the pieces come from the first cut—that's why they're so cheap. I purchase a truckload for about twenty dollars. The actual delivery is a surprise—six- to eight-foot long slabs, two-inch–thick sections of bark and wood, the first cuts made by the saw that changes the shape of a log from round to square.

Slabs sticking out in every direction, the huge truck and its contents rumble up on the street below. I'm supposed to unload it with the driver. Fortunately, the garage is on the street level underneath the big room. It takes us four hours to unload and it's not a neat job. Stacking and arranging these long pieces is impossible in my debilitated state and the driver is eager to depart, so we chuck the pieces into the garage, filling it up to the fifteen-foot ceiling. Neatness will be restored as I work my way through the pile carrying boards up the interior stairs to the big room. The fireplace is up to any length they deliver, so I'm warm for the winter.

Exhausted, I build a fire and cook to celebrate the arrival of the wood. I bake a fish, with rice and spinach. I am at a point where even the slightest excess of food makes my eyes bulge and my capillaries red. Food is the final addiction. In remembrance of Michelle Rubin, I vow to reduce my diet to brown rice, fruit and vegetables. I try to settle down and relax. But there's too much to contend with. I'm at the edge of the void. That's where this process is leading me, right over the edge. I get my journal out and begin to write: *sex, alcohol, food, drugs, power, gambling, sports, money, nostalgia, friends, shopping.* I write about all the worldly pleasures I've abandoned, but what comes out on paper is a diatribe against these things. I feel like a prisoner and prisoners aren't allowed the luxury of addiction. Abruptly, from one day to the next, I am inside a new life, all my little escapes no longer available.

I spend about fifty francs a week on food—it's all my Solex can carry—mostly vegetables, fruit, cheese, fish and olive oil. The bakery in St. Jean is renowned for its crispy, crunchy *Pain*—I don't have to take up space for bread in the Solex saddlebags. Funny, when I'm among people in the market it's as if I'm invisible. Unlike Paris where I played the charming expatriate, here among the crowded market stalls, I observe people's moods and habits from the outside in. They don't see me. I am a fourth-dimension creature who causes heads to turn, like a sudden chill wind. It's like watching a TV monitor in a store window. People moving back and forth across the screen, turning their heads, and then zipping out of frame. Even the pretty girls make no impression. I respond to nothing except the obsession inside me. Ride in on my Solex—a specter cloaked in US Army surplus—turn the heads of respectable people, then ride on out again. Yes, I do turn heads, but so engrossed in my meditation, I pay no attention to it.

Each morning I sit on the hook rug in my bedroom with my eyes closed, meditating. I am aware of the flow of air. It is like a gentle wind inside me and I can hear it and feel its effervescence as a soft summer breeze. It's a new sensation, and that for me is everything, because I hang on the slightest change like a lost and becalmed mariner waiting for a rising wind.

• • •

Observing my breath as I sit one morning, I am aware that it has the property of direction. At each inhalation the hitherto imperceptible wind in my belly appears to eddy slightly at the bottom of my abdomen as it descends before taking an upward circular course. Or so it appears to me. Down the back, then up the front, in a circular motion.

Something clicks. I remember the words 'backward-flowing method' in *The Secret of the Golden Flower*. Words I've passed over a hundred times, never having a clue as to what they meant, never imagining they might be important. I break off to look for the passage. In two quick flips, I've located the text, "At this time one works at the energy with the purpose of making it flow backward and rise, flow down to fall like the upward spinning of the sun-wheel…in this way one succeeds in bringing the true energy to its original place. This is the backward-flowing method."[20]

I decide to let the venerable *I Ching* guide me. When I open the book, my three 20 centimes coins fall out and roll around. I total up the numbers, two heads and a tail equals eight, a young yang in the first place. I toss again, three heads, a yang line, then four more tosses until I have:

34. TA CHUANG / The Power of the Great

The hexagram points to a time when inner worth mounts with great force and comes to power. But its strength has already passed beyond the median line, hence there is a danger that one may rely entirely on one's own power and forget to ask what is right.

But the latter objection is addressed by the fortuitous appearance of a nine in the second place:

Nine in the second place means:
Perseverance brings good fortune.

The premise here is that the gates to success are beginning to open. Resistance gives way and we forge ahead.

I close the *I Ching* and sit on my bedroom mat. I must decide: Either go with the 'backward-flowing method' or stop altogether. There is no turning back. Truly, the tiger by the tail, the bull by the horns, a fish jumping out of water.

I visualize a plumb-line and close my eyes. I command the breath to change direction and it obeys. I am elated at receiving confirmation from the book. What I don't yet realize is that this is the last time I will direct the meditation process. From now on I am on automatic pilot. I remember the words of Ram Dass: *At first, you do it; later, it does you.* Action to attain non-action.

For a week I observe my breath circulate in the opposite direction without noticing any effect. The mind goes on autopilot and I go back to my uninspired routine: walking, cooking, meditating.

Then, two weeks later, about the length of time it takes the back-ward-flowing process to become permanent, there's something new. On the day in question, I feel a sensation at the base of my spine like the cracking of a small egg and the spilling out of its contents. For the next month, I observe the fluid-like contents of the egg trickle out of its reservoir and slowly begin to climb my spine. What is this fluid? I can't describe it exactly. It seems to emanate from the base of the spine and press upward. Each time I sit to meditate, it has risen a half an inch higher.

A bone appears in my chest; it stretches laterally from the sternum around to my back, the second rib on the left side. Why has it been in the wrong position all these years? It appears to be straightening my shoulders while increasing the size of my chest cavity. I have been touching my body and my head since I started meditating because I've had a strange feeling that it was changing, like in a timed-release Doctor Jekyll experiment, and I am a New-Age Mr. Hyde.

I am elated and begin to tell myself that soon it will be over. It'll rise to the third eye, there'll be a tremendous shock, an explosion, and I will be transported into an entirely new realm of consciousness.

• • •

A few days later I start to observe new activity. During medita-tion I notice my breath 'splitting' into two streams—one on the left and one on the right side of my body. More curious, the streams are operating in separate channels from my head to my abdomen.

What is this? I wonder. Certainly, not good. It's not easy to describe the kind of incremental stumbling forward that occurs during my meditation. Sitting with legs crossed, I make up words to describe the indescribable, comparing each incremental difference with what happened before I reversed the direction of my breath. Only by comparison can I understand the subtle changes. Previously, my abdomen descended, drawing the air inside. Now there seems to be two abdomens, two respiratory tracts. The muscles that control the two sides don't function as a locked pair. One side draws in more air, then expels it at a different rate. If, on exhalation, the muscles of the abdomen act independently, then one side will become more developed than the other.

This is disquieting. But by now, I am used to surprises. A few days ago, I could have given up meditation for good. But I chose to continue, and now I can't go back—the backward-flowing method cannot be reversed. That choice, even as of one week ago, no longer exists. And I realize that the inside of me is filled with pieces that interlock and work together like a well-oiled machine.

• • •

I've been invited for dinner at Isabelle's. The first thing I notice about Marc Bonet is that his eyes don't glaze over when I tell him what I'm doing. In fact, he wants to hear more. We split off from the group. Céline, Marc's wife, huddles with Gabriel, Isabelle's husband, discussing the ins and outs of some business deal.

Marc has a car and wants to come down to St. Jean the next day to talk with me. I tell him that I stay away from people—not from any social disinclination, but because my meditation demands solitude.

"Do you think I'm crazy?" I ask.

Marc's a bit shook up by the question; he's only known me for an hour.

"Gabriel does," I continue.

"That's what I want to talk to you about."

"I'm not crazy. I'm here because I can be alone. I don't have to offer excuses for my appearance."

"We're going to be here for four months," he says. "What you're doing…whatever it is…I understand. Céline won't, but she'll feel you…if you know what I mean."

"Looks like she's getting an earful from Gabriel," I say, nodding toward the huddle.

9—Surrender

No, the crisis I was passing through was not a creation of my own imagination. It had a real physiological basis and was interwoven with the whole organic structure of my body. The entire machinery from the brain to the smallest organ was involved, and there was no escape for me from the storm of nervous forces which blew through my system day and night.[21]

> ~ *Kundalini: The Evolutionary Energy in Man*—Gopi Krishna

arc comes down to St. Jean to talk the next afternoon. He tells me that he and Céline have decided the property deal won't work. They'll stay as long as it takes to settle their business, then it's home to Canada. He says he wants to help me.

Céline is also prepared to help me even though she doesn't understand and is disturbed by my appearance. In fact, when Marc tells Isabelle that he is going to invite me to live in their house if things get rough, Gabriel tells him I am going to die and not to associate with me. Evidently, my appearance the other night shocked him.

"Marc," I say, "I'm going to get worse before I get better, but I'm not going to die. I can live on one teaspoon of yogurt and a few sesame seeds a day...then hike up the mountain. If anything, I have *too much* energy."

"If it gets bad, stay with us," he says.

•   •   •

I am looking forward to springtime with the hope that it will bring closure, as if nature's renewed vitality will finish this process. As the season progresses, however, my condition takes a turn. By June, three months have elapsed since I reversed my breath, over a year since I began meditation. I am getting worse and better at the same time; only the worse part is much worse. I'm taking "the better" on faith. At the same time, I can't believe that I am so completely helpless.

It's not the meditation. It's when I'm up and around, puttering in the house that I imagine my one step forward–two steps back evolution is due to bad karma. I get these notions from reading spiritual books. To stay focused, I try to limit speculation, telling myself that notions gleaned from books, no matter how *spiritual*, are useless. Nothing matters except breathing in and out—my experience, and how I manage it. Everything else just feeds the inner dialogue. So what if I filled a storehouse with a lifetime of bad karma—so did Milarepa. The important thing is to move forward.

Some nights I am unable to sleep. I read late, but cannot concentrate with the energy staging for its nightly thrust up the spine.

Soon it will be into my head and I reckon that a major upheaval will occur. One cup of yogurt, an apple and a bowl of rice are now sufficient nourishment for a whole day. In fact, most of the time, even these meager quantities are too much.

As I meditate each morning, my whole body radiates a kind of glowing energy. It isn't the Circulation of the Light, which, according to the book, is the ultimate goal.

"The Golden Flower is the light…The work on the circulation of the light depends entirely on the backward-flowing method, so that the thoughts (the place of heavenly consciousness, the heavenly heart) are gathered together. The heavenly heart lies between the sun and the moon (i.e. between the two eyes)."[22]

The spinal energy will be crashing in on the heavenly heart (the third eye), sometime during the month of July, I figure. According to a dream, it'll be July 9th. I cast the *I Ching*. Even the most unscientific divination is better than none at all. But hey, I'm a believer now.

  1. CH'IEN / The Creative

The first hexagram is made up of six unbroken lines. These unbroken lines stand for the primal power, which is light-giving, active, strong, and of the spirit.

Nine the second place means;
Dragon appearing in the field.
It furthers one to see the great man.

Here the effects of the light-giving power begin to manifest themselves.

As the energy ascends to my brain, ever-smaller morsels of food bring rapid expansion and painful contraction. I go to bed cursing my birth, after spending the most difficult day of my life.

I'm not tired, even after fasting the whole day. In fact, I'm invigorated, primed, ready to walk the hills. I pop a single sesame seed into my mouth. Immediately, the energy at the coccyx surges up the spine. This is the first day of my adult life that I have not eaten—except for a single grain of sesame.

The following day my body shakes and trembles painfully. A kind of valve opens in my head allowing the energy to surge up the middle of my spine and into my brain. Something conclusive is happening. The pain stops and my breathing becomes unified—as long as I concentrate on my forehead, on the place between the two eyes—the heavenly heart.

I completely reread *The Secret of the Golden Flower*, finding nothing specific about my present condition. I'm ready to react at the slightest sign of abnormality. I only hope I don't panic.

In my recent journal entries the scrawl has become loopier and more irregular, reflecting an inability to concentrate even to the point of holding a pen.

June 25, 1973—St. Jean, L'Herault

I am not prepared through Yoga, psychology, or religion. I am like a third-rate Faust who stumbled backward through the Doors of Perception. I have played leapfrog with life and may not come through this. Why can't I accept that I am just going mad?

The next day, rereading that passage, I cannot remember what I meant to say. In a word, I am delirious, incapable of writing. There are all these experiences I want to set down on paper, but my mind, like my handwriting, is too chaotic. As for the elementary rules of structure, I can't remember them. Finally, I put down the pen for good. How can a pilot write as his rocket plummets toward impact? I'll have to write from memory—after the crash.

This day extends into the next, and the next. I lose track of the days. I am locked down to my bed, mute witness to the battle in my head. I pace, I meditate, I read, but I do not sleep or eat. What is a day? When does it end? I do not know the answer, cannot repeat the question. I am dying. My body is being snatched. I am invaded by an alien force. Helpless, I nevertheless resist. But the battlements are being overrun; it's hopeless.

Hungry, sleepless, reckless, determined, enthralled. No longer the desperate pilot, I am a passenger. As the cockpit rolls back and forth, I watch the controls move by themselves. Whoever is flying this vessel is doing a better job than I ever could. Sotto voce, I repeat: *I'm going to crash; I'm going to explode.* As if hurtling through some kind of barrier—heat, sonic, light, all at once—the cockpit rattles and shakes; it is falling apart. And I with it. Undulating, my body writhes and shakes. *Am I in my bed, or floating above it, all the time shaking and wondering who is controlling me? What Power?*

Is this a religious experience? Doesn't religious experience include this type of purification? Fasting, sleeplessness, deprivation. Christ in the desert—Buddha under the Bodhi tree. All I can do is observe and not do anything stupid.

• • •

The *Solex* climbs toward St. Privat, winding windward over the twisting mountain road. Dark canyon shadows alternate with bright sunny stretches. From sunshine, into shadow, into the sun again. No time for the eyes to adjust. A simple flick of the wrist and it's all over. Hit a pothole and forget to straighten the wheel. A moment's inattention, and I'm lying at the bottom of a dark canyon among scrub oak and sycamore. Remnants that won't be found for months.

• • •

When I arrive in St. Privat, I beg Marc to drive me to the American Hospital in Paris.

"It's happening all wrong," I say.

"You have to surrender."

"I almost drove off the road," I say. "Into a canyon."

"But something wouldn't let you," he says.

"Yes."

"You, yourself!"

"Me?"

"You're not meant to end up at the bottom of a ravine, man. I know about these things. You've been singled out."

Marc leads me upstairs to the guest room and in the twilight we sit facing each other in the lotus position, staring into each other's eyes. All at once he starts to glow, assuming the shape and coloring of a Chinese sage—like one of the drawings in *The Secret of the Golden Flower*. A colorful energy field radiates from his head and shoulders. He rises, seems to float toward me, raps me twice on the crown of the head then leaves the room. Exhaustion overtakes me and I lie down.

Marc comes back and covers me with a blanket. The *I Ching* I cast that morning was emphatic: Stop struggling and submit, it said. So I do—more from exhaustion than choice. I lie in Marc's house, watching the sound and light show in my head, making no effort to control it. Valves open like solenoids, causing nerves and muscles to strain like the strings of a weaver's loom.

As the third eye battles for ascendancy, a hole opens in my abdomen and a force field of energy shoots out, following an arced trajectory outside my body to my head. A castanet-shaped gland in my head opens to receive its stream of energy. I can feel the muscle walls at my solar plexus pull apart and open. I feel the energy shimmering forth.

This dazzling display lasts about five minutes. Then two spear-like things—extensions of my nose, it seems—gang up on the castanet-like gland and try to pull it down. My entire head moves and twists uncontrollably as the muscles and nerves wind in all directions. But the gland will not be pushed and, climbing still further, it squirms and pushes its way into a space between the two halves of my brain.

Once this happens, the battle stops and all, including the two tentacles, cease struggling. And this gland, or Chakra, the third eye—whatever its rightful name—turns like a gyroscope, meting out instructions and assigning tasks. Probes touch specific locations in my brain, causing muscles throughout my body to react. It controls the elixir, directing it to designated locations. No longer chaotic, it's very precise; a factory at work. All organs, nerves, glands—even the spear-like tentacles—snap to attention, ready to serve.

I know—I've seen it. Under vibrant illumination, I've followed every movement as if I was watching a brain scan from within.

• • •

I wake up in Marc's house with the statuettes of a kiwi bird and a little man seated on a long-extinct dodo staring at me. Something has taken me over. After several minutes of lying on my back, I realize I am lucid. The commotion in my head has stopped.

Then the wonderment comes howling back. It seems the great metaphysical riddle of the ages has converged in me. Yet throughout my ordeal, no voices whispered to me—I was not called by the voice of some personal sponsor. The endless pitter-patter dialogues were just that, not voices from a burning bush.

Something within has steered me to a safe harbor. For my own good, it kept me from eating, from sleeping, from drugging myself. It knew what my body should be doing at every moment. And I tuned into it just in time. Lucky, because it obliterates resistance.

Already, during these half-awake first moments, I have a sense of it. It is machine-like: valves, levers and buttons controlled by the monitor between the eyes. It has begun remaking me without heed for my former life—that's gone forever. A new being is taking shape. And there is no one out there waiting to take credit at this quintessential Hollywood moment. No Color by Technicolor. No credit roll. It came from a book.

I try to remember the lost, threadless days, racking my mind for details. How did I end up at Marc's? At first, it's rather hazy. I want to write it down. Struggling a bit, I finally sit up. But my memory is hidden in a tide of sleepless nights. Then it hits me. Not eating. Days without food. *I'm in the kitchen, reaching for a yogurt and I stop. I resolve not to eat until it's over. Kill or heal me—I'm past caring.*

I remember being hungry, at the same time curiously unperturbed by the lack of food. I remember writing in my journal. Oh yes, the gland in the middle of my forehead. I remember holding it there for days—like a juggler whose life depends on not dropping a single pin. Rolling my eyes upward and writhing until I consider getting on the Solex and riding to Clérmont L'Herault to buy a bottle of the meanest whiskey I can procure, drinking it down to end the struggle.

It comes back. The climbing into bed, wrapping myself up. Not being able to sleep because the gland is on the top of my nose, stifling my breathing. Dozing off, I start to sputter. Waking up, unsure of where I am. Days without sleep, weeks of fasting. Not a grain of rice, only water. Violent exercise and meditation all day long to stabilize my breathing.

I recall a sweet taste spilling into the back of my mouth. I can still taste it—a honey-like elixir. I remember looking in *The Secret of the Golden Flower*, trying to find a reference. According to the book, it's the magic elixir of life.

I remember being able to see inside my head, seeing the gland between my eyes open like a castanet to catch the elixir. The gland, in turn, sprays it on my brain. I see how the elixir revives me, gives me strength. How I struggle to resist. How I fail to realize it is saving my life. The crazy thoughts. Suicide, frontal lobotomy, insanity. Buying a large bottle of wine from the proprietor at the little café in St. Jean. His turning white from fear when I enter the bar, how he gives me the wine without asking for money. How he shuns me as if I'm carrying a contagious disease. How I put the wine on the kitchen counter. How I go to the bedroom to meditate, feeling hopelessly overwhelmed.

●　●　●

After ten days, I'm eating plentiful amounts of food, followed by rest, then more food. My head is cracking, reshaping. How is this possible? I don't know. But it's cracking. I can feel it. I can hear the pings and pops. Previously, there was a ridge down the length of my skull. But the front portion of the skull is flat now; the ridge is now confined to the back.

The force I've unleashed is rebalancing the two sides of my person. Is this why Michelle Rubin gave me that book? Did she somehow recognize my lack of symmetry? Did she realize that the shape of the head controls the shape of the body? Well, it does. I can see it when I lay down, see how the force is pushing my head to fill the dimensions of its template overlay. And once the head is perfect, so will the body be.

At the speed things are moving, it seems like it will take only a few days, yet I fear it's a prodigious undertaking and I temper my elation with caution.

I sleep well. I am constantly hungry, but I have to be careful not to overeat, which for me can be measured in one sesame seed too many. I can no longer meditate in the lotus position; it has to be done on my back, lying like a baby unaware that growth is taking place while it sleeps.

I am a new person. My anxiety is gone, and the traumatic physical routine of fasting and insomnia ends the moment I wake up at Marc's. I am in good hands and I feel great.

As soon as I lie down, no matter the time of day, energy surges into my head. The best moments, however, are late afternoon, around 5:00 or 6:00 p.m. Yes, the power is always there and it's clearly up to something. I do not struggle; I have surrendered completely. But what is it up to? It has a purpose; that much is certain.

Throughout the day, Céline brings me small quantities of yogurt, grains and fruit. Intuitively, I know what to eat. It's like a nightmare chapter has ended and a new, happier one has begun. I am amazed at the transition from starving myself and being tossed by inner torment to a smooth landing. I am able to sleep, without torment or energy overload. I think back to my first reading of *The Secret of the Golden Flower*. How impenetrable it first seemed. But I cracked its esoteric codes without consulting doctors or gurus. By miracle or by chance, everything has turned out right. I can feel my body being cleansed and restored; I can see the blueprint of my perfect body.

The next morning, I lie in bed fantasizing on the future, thinking how great it would be if I could just sit back on the Enlightenment Express, watching the light circulate and waiting for sublime spiritual transformation.

> Every separate thought takes shape and becomes visible in color and form.
> The total spiritual power unfolds its traces and transforms itself into emptiness.

Going out into being and going out into non-being, one completes the miraculous Tao.
All separate shapes appear as bodies, united with a true source.[23]

While I lie there, the energy continues to push outward against the entire inner surface of my skull, and by extension, into my body. After an hour, the pressure increases to such a degree that I start to pitch and roll. My shoulders circle back then forward in rapid involuntary movements while my hands, like artificial limbs, lift then drop onto my belly and rub in swift circular motions.

In my mind's eye, I see it all. It's as if the perfect causal body lies like a template shroud over its physical counterpart and through some type of transformational magnetism, causes the physical entity to swell to the infinite proportions of the causal. *As if…as if…I'm always saying as if.* As if there's no other way to describe what's happening except by metaphors, which usually miss their mark.

When I awake from my meditative slumber, my body has shrunk back to its previous state—only not quite. It is like a balloon that's being inflated in stages, growing infinitesimally larger by degrees. Some new muscle or nerve or hidden channel is activated and contributes its resources to the rebuilding. I am witnessing my own retrofitting. Yes, I would like to be catapulted into the loftier regions of enlightenment, but I have some repairs to do. Before addressing spiritual growth and lofty questions of expanded consciousness, the Kundalini must rewire my nervous system and reengineer my body.

10—Awakening

Within our six-foot body we must strive for the form that existed before the laying down of heaven and earth.[24]

- *The Secret of the Golden Flower*—Lu Yen - Richard Wilhelm, Translator

I lie in bed recovering, feeling like an autistic child who suddenly awakens from the spell of an unrelenting demon. I now realize I have to learn the ways of the real world. I understand nothing—neither social discourse, economics, job skills, nor family relations. All have been buried; I'm not sure where. Anyway, I have to start over.

After ten more days of pampering by Marc and Céline, I am feeling back to normal—with one exception, of course. As soon as I lie down, the energy takes possession of my body. Its purpose is clear. Willingly, I defer to its healing power. For that is what it is: the healing power of nature. Having abdicated its throne at birth to the conscious mind, it has once again ascended to the place of primacy. It knows what to do. It's the only part of my being that does. For unfortunately, while I'm awake, the mind still influences the decisions I make. And I realize I'm living between two worlds. I am past thirty-five and have no future. What can I do in the real world?

I am under no delusion; the two sides of my body are unequal and, although a tremendous force is at work, the retrofit will take time. But what a formidable array of tools it has. It pushes buttons and opens valves in my brain, and the corresponding muscles of my solar plexus part with an involuntary stretching effort and streams of energy that feel like an invisible fountain flow in a shimmering, arc-like trajectory toward the third eye. Even though I can find no description in any of my sources, this substance reminds me of purified Prana, the life-force energy. Unlike the elixir of life though, I find no mention or description of it in *The Secret of the Golden Flower*.

What I haven't realized is how close to the edge I came. After my fifteen-day fast and ten nights of sleep deprivation, I have lost about fifty pounds.

I write letters to Margo, my father and other friends. Text copied from my journal and personalized. Putting it into words isn't easy. Only by writing and rewriting am I able to straighten out the chronology.

• • •

I help Marc and Céline clean out their house and pack. I ride the Solex back to St. Jean, grateful for the concern they have shown me. The first thing I do is pour the unopened contents of the large bottle of wine down the sink.

A week later I accompany Marc and Céline to the airport in Marseilles. Marc leaves me his 1967 Burgundy-colored Renault *Quatrelle*, a mini-station wagon—like the *Deux Chevaux*—one of the icons of the French roadway. On the way back I stop in Montpellier to buy clothes.

Figure 2: Before Kundalini   *Figure 3*: After Kundalini

Outside the shop there's a Photomat and I'm thinking that I haven't taken a photograph in a long time. When the pictures drop out and I get a load of them, I nearly pass out. I've been avoiding mirrors and now realize why. At home I hold my new photo next to one taken in Paris a few months before I left. If the eyes are the windows to the soul, I'm damned.

•   •   •

Freshly equipped with wheels, I spend time re-adjusting to the world. I eat pizza in the café. The hills and mountains I explored on foot, I now cover by motorcar. How much it resembles Arizona, this forgotten red dirt corridor of Languedoc.

Soon, I am strong enough to practice Hatha Yoga again. My biggest problem is diet. I tend to eat too much, not from gluttony, but because the Kundalini demands it. I have a huge appetite that makes it hard to stop loading my plate. I can eat anything and frequently do. The problem is, later on, when I lie down, the force runs out of control.

On a typical day my breakfast consists of dried prunes, apple juice, cornbread, yogurt and an orange. For lunch I eat rye bread with sheep's cheese, some olives and vegetable juice. My dinner consists of brown rice & peas, carrots & zucchini and a salad. Not much by ordinary standards. And although I'm trying to follow a basic vegetarian diet, I nibble away throughout the day, losing track of total consumption. It's as if my Kundalini is calling for food, yet I'm unsure of what to feed it.

Two weeks later, lying down for my evening session with the Kundalini, I slip into a trance-like state. Immediately, I see myself, not as I am today, but as the perfect boy I was before my accident. My alter ego comes forth to kiss my forehead and speak to me.

"You've almost undone what you did to me," says the vision.

"What did I do?" I ask.

"You know what you did, how you let the splinter fester inside me."

And I see Christ's passion set to music by a seven-year-old soloist in the choir, the glory of the springtime Cantata echoing among the timber spars of the chapel. And I am there again, as that boy. The whole chapel is watching me sing. At that instant, I know the truth. How I lost my singing voice, my tennis ability, my prowess at math. I remember the numbers dancing before me, and I realize that by letting the splinter fester in my ankle, I crippled that boy. In one blinding moment, the past comes crashing into the present. But it's too big for the present.

"Will I ever be rid of the splinter?" I ask him.

"Be patient," he says. "You found the one way in an entire universe to make amends for what you did. For that you should be thankful."

I start to shake. The force grips my shoulders, rotating them in tight circles, first together, then in opposition. As I writhe in bed, my right arm rises, drops to my stomach, and starts to rub it in swift circular motions. My left foot sinks down below my right and rubs the sole of my foot. Then my right foot takes a turn at it. My toenails dig into my soles.

A few moments later, everything stops and I lie still once again. I feel a force surging up from my loins. *What will happen when I get back to the world and want to be with a woman? Conflict? Avoidance? I know it will happen. But how will I cope?*

The first passage I run across that night:

> Yang wei rises from the outer side of the foot about one and a half inches below the ankle, goes up the outer side of the leg and after skirting the back of the body, enters the upper arm, halfway along which it veers to the shoulder, the neck, and then behind the ear; it connects thirty-two psychic centers.[25]

Yes, the splinter entered right at the *Yang wei*, shutting down nerve conduits to 32 psychic centers in my body. I turn the pages, looking for something on sublimation. I run across plenty of references to involuntary movements, but nothing conclusive on sublimation and how to deal with sexual desire. I'll cross that bridge when I come to it.

At the moment, I am devouring my meager supply of books: *The Fourth Way*, Ouspensky; *History of Philosophy*, Bertrand Russell; *The Tin Drum*; *Anna Karenina*; *Be Here Now*; *The Doors of Perception*, Aldous Huxley; *The Bhagavad Gita*; a book on Edgar Cayce; *The Life of Milarepa*; *The Secrets of Chinese Meditation*; *Thus Spake Zarathustra*; *The Life of the Buddha*; *The Master Game*, the book my father gave me.

• • •

At the end of September I load everything into the *Quatrelle* and start for Paris. My worldly possessions fit into the back of a *Quatrelle* with room to spare. Can I continue to live without a lot of stuff? Won't last, but it feels good—owning nothing except the contents of a *Quatrelle*. I think about the junk Margo and I accumulated—the stuff she gave away and how I sulked. A hundred times the contents of the *Quatrelle*.

Instead of the Autoroute I take the back roads, straight up the Massif Central, through the little towns most tourists avoid. Lodève, Millau, St. Flour, Clermont-Ferrand, Moulins where I pick up the N7, then across the Loire at Nevers, and on to Paris via Montargis, Nemours, and Fontainebleau. Climbing out of Lodève onto the flat moonscape of the Larzac plateau and into the lush green hills of the Massif, I stop in St. Flour to buy a hunk of indigenous Cantal cheese, the best hard cheese in France. Twelve non-stop hours. But stop I must, especially after double clutching my way over mountains in an altitude challenged *Quatrelle*. Cheese, bread, apple juice, and eyefuls of beauty, my meager fare for the trip. After a year of retreat, it's invigorating to be out in the world again.

I am unable to find a hotel in Paris, so I call Genvième, a lady I met before leaving for St. Jean. Don't know why I thought of her. Must have been the time we'd met at the American Center, the day she'd overwhelmed me with her chatter on spiritual transformation. So, I'm thinking that maybe we should catch up. She invites me to stay at her house. I'm heading back to the states, I tell her. Come along anyway, until you leave. Just sold my car, I tell her.

"At the Gare St. Lazare, take the train to Bernay," she says. "I'll pick you up."

"Alright, okay," I say.

"I'm anxious to hear about what's been happening."

On the way I check Galignani's. At last, something substantial, a book paralleling my own experience. I devour Gopi Krishna's *Kundalini: The Evolutionary Energy in Man* during the two-hour train ride to Bernay.

I find Genvième lonely and impatient. Hearing about my ordeal is the furthest thing from her mind. The hour-by-hour actuality of my ascetic routine—frequent meditation, yogurt with sesame seeds, infuriates her. Outwardly, she is polite. Inside, she's seething. It's sure to boil over. For dinner, she insists on preparing a big meal.

Geneviève is so verbal. I'm not used to talking. After three hours at the dinner table my throat gives out; I literally can't talk. She thinks it's some kind of ploy for avoiding conversation.

Not that her conversation relates to me; it's mostly one-sided self-justification—about her marriage, her ex-husband, her lonely life. It's the same for me, for all of us, I say. That's what life produces: fabulous, self-justification machines. She doesn't want my insights on life. She looks at me with such loathing. At first I can't figure out why she's so pissed.

"Geneviève," I rasp, "that was a great meal. I'd like to meditate. I can feel the energy building up."

"You don't know what this is all about, do you?" She looks at me with such disbelief, as if I'd just coughed up a frog.

I stand there for a moment, feeling stupid. "Boy, am I dumb."

"You don't remember how you looked at me last year when we met at the Center? If you'd talked bee-keeping, I'd have been at the library looking up tupelo and orange blossom. That's how bad the tingle was."

"You mean all this, the meditation, etcetera, was just talk…"

"Hey," she says, "first things first."

"Yeah, first things first. Only my first thing is meditation. I don't look at women that way anymore, not even beautiful women like yourself."

"That is such a lot of crap. If you don't want to, just say so."

"Let me read you something."

"I'll listen to anything, just so long as you don't expect me to believe it."

I try to clear my throat. My voice is like the stripped gears of the *Quatrelle*. "'I viewed this unnatural disappearance of a deep-rooted feeling with despondency, finding myself a different man altogether and my unhappiness increased at seeing myself robbed of that which gives life its greatest charm.'[26] Gopi Krishna's the only human being who's kept a record. Pow, suddenly no sexual feelings. It's impossible to understand if you haven't experienced it."

"I can understand someone living another reality. Schizophrenics do," she replied.

"Yeah, I guess you could say it's a form of schizophrenia."

"Maybe it'll turn you into some kind of superman, a guy who can go all night."

"I'm not used to being so emotionally...I don't know... detached. Like the place where I used to feel love, anger, pride, even desire, has been cut out of me."

"I can't influence you, not even by showing a little *décolletage*," she says in reference to her peasant blouse. "And you can't convince me."

"Genviève, do you meditate?"

"I tried Yoga, meditation, books, Tai Chi classes. Not like you; you're into it. That doesn't mean I don't take it seriously."

"I'm sorry for being so...so wrapped up in my own thing. My life was a mess."

She comes over to where I'm washing the dishes and squeezes me into a bear hug. The duration makes me uncomfortable, especially when I look down and see the shine in her eyes.

When I tell her definitively that I can't handle sex, she says, "You can stay here as long as you want; I don't care."

Whew, it's going to be difficult talking to people about my experience. So, I'm simply not going to try. I'm on the train back to Paris when it dawns on me. I should have packed up immediately, the moment I realized how she felt, and not stayed the extra two days.

I spend the next week filling in my journal. A daunting task. I'm still not sure about what I am seeing inside my head. The once-bright light is now partially extinguished. Nevertheless, when I lie down each evening, the power surges to the fore. The show goes on; the involuntary movements, the pings and pops, my head cracking and reshaping, but the magic elixir and the Pranic flow from the solar plexus only happen when I feel weak or sick.

11—Adjustment

The opinion of 10,000 men is of no value if none of them know anything about the subject.

~ Marcus Aurelius

I leave Paris precipitously at the end of October—after dreaming about my father. In the dream, he's run out of gas and is stopped on the side of the road. I am on my way to meet him, driving at top speed down a sloping hill on a long barren road with no trees or buildings on either side. In what seems to be dream hours of driving, I see this little dot of a car, always the same size. It takes forever to get to where he is. Suddenly, I am alongside his car with its hood raised. Then I wake up, immediately realizing that something is wrong and I must get on a plane.

In Palm Beach, I deplane on the tarmac. My father is standing off to one side. In the unforgiving Florida sunlight, I see what triggered my dream. Frailer, with few traces of his former vigor, he appears shrunken, his shirt collar too big, his grip not nearly as powerful. Embarrassed by the black rings that circle his eyes, he quickly puts on sunglasses and leads me to his car.

Seeing my father like this brings tears to my eyes. I hold myself ready to remonstrate if he betrays the merest sign of weakness, but none is tendered. Perhaps it's just being held in check behind dark glasses.

In the car headed down to Delray Beach, under questioning, he tells me he fell asleep on the beach one morning, then, as the sun began to boil, he suffered a stroke, lying there unconscious for hours under the noonday sun. Passersby, unaware that anything was wrong with the sleeping sunbather, went about their business—building sand castles and splashing in the tidewater. Not until a neighbor came along for his afternoon dip did anyone talk to him. Realizing he was paralyzed and unconscious, the neighbor summoned the paramedics. His recitation over, he is finally in tears. This is the only time I've seen my father cry.

He whips out a pack of cigarettes and lights up. "Aren't cigarettes bad for you?" I ask. "With your condition…"

"I can't quit."

"What do you mean?"

"I can't stop. I tried." Overtaxed kidneys, brought on by the stroke, he says about the black circles under his eyes.

"What about that book on AA you were going to write?"

"I got down here, never started it."

"That's when you do things like that…in retirement. So what do you do?"

"Play golf."

"You still go to meetings?"

He looks at me intently. "I'll never stop going to meetings." Then he seems to lose concentration.

"Good," I mutter. "By the way, I read *The Master Game*. I was hoping you'd be writing your own follow up."

Being under scrutiny makes him uncomfortable. He changes the subject back to me and my prodigal ways—as if my questions amount to censure. *I feel like saying, relax, your fathering days are over. It's my turn to play the parent.*

With a glazed expression, he listens to my vague account of the last two years. I keep it vague on purpose. I can see the stroke has squeezed every last bit of spiritual curiosity out of him. I guess that's what happens when the doctors finally take over.

• • •

Our relationship is going nowhere. Now that he has dropped his pet book project, we don't have much to talk about. There is only golf. And golf is not on my roadmap. I see his illness, feel his pain. I imagined that I might help him. At least he still plays golf. For once, I regret that he's too weak to attack me with his former gusto.

"What are you going to do now, film editing?" He has contacts in New York and offers to pay a week at the Sutton Hotel.

"I can't go back to film editing," I tell him, "not with what's happening inside me."

"It's your imagination," he says.

"It's real," I insist. He looks at me like I am a talking weasel.

"I'm on my way to DC," I announce. "I'll stay with Roper then work my way back into things over time. My future involves Kundalini. It may take me a while to get it together, but in the end, that's what I have to do. You must know the feeling from AA."

"You have to get back to work," he says.

"I know. I want to."

"When?"

"My body will tell me. Shouldn't it be like that?" I ask. *To be confident enough to listen to your inner self.* He gives up. I am speaking a strange, unintelligible language.

He wants me to drive him to North Carolina so he can escape the Florida heat and insists that I get some new clothes to be more presentable on the golf course—double-knit, Polyester slacks and sports shirts are in fashion. They grate my neck, and I look ridiculous with my long beard and emaciated body. Three days later, we take off for North Carolina.

I stay with him in Asheville for ten days, hoping to get him settled. Nothing seems to please him. I don't know if it's me, my staring at him every time he lights up a cigarette, or just some end game funk. We change rooms three times, then finally hotels. Something about a noise in the corridor, he says. The next night, I read until 3:00 a.m. and never hear a thing. In the morning, he tells me they were making noise all night. So, I strike a deal with a start-up motel run by two young people from Raleigh. We take a little cabin and eat the good meals they serve. He plays golf and I practice Yoga and read. I ask him if he wants to learn Yoga. It might help with his smoking, I suggest. He makes a joke about Gandhi and the Indian rope trick.

• • •

The first thing I do in New York is go straight to Samuel Weiser's bookstore, the city's spiritual watering hole. Next to Galignani's, it's apocryphal. Loads of spiritual books. I snap up Gopi Krishna's *The Biological Basis of Religion and Genius.* I want to find writings from other mystical traditions, something closer to my own origins than the Taoist texts I've been following. But while reading his book in the confines of the Sutton Hotel, I come across this:

The statements of the kind that during the process the semen dries up with suction and becomes thin, that the male organ shrinks, or that the sexual appetite is lost, contained in old manuals, cannot fail to convey important bits of information to the modern savants engaged in the investigation.

> An ancient Chinese work, ***The Secret of the Golden Flower***, contains unmistakable hints about this process, which no one with some knowledge of this process can fail to notice, and yet Jung, in his commentary on the book, entirely preoccupied with his own theories about the unconscious, despite the unambiguous nature of the statements in the work, finds in it only material for the corroboration of his own ideas and nothing beyond that.[27]

Yes, I remember reading Jung's commentary and quickly tiring of it because it contained no empirical information, only a long-winded attempt to correlate his theories on animus and anima with the notions of Yin and Yang. And that's fine if you don't want to do anything except talk and debate. Why didn't they ask someone who had actually deciphered the secrets and practiced the method to write an updated version of the commentary? Gopi Krishna, for instance! I vow to stick with the empirical Taoist approach. Born in ancient China, refined in the mountains of Tibet, these people were doers, not dabblers. *The Secret of the Golden Flower* is only 44 pages and its companion piece, *The Book of Consciousness and Life*, only 9 pages. Jung's Commentary, on the other hand, rambles on for 54 pages.

I agree with Gopi Krishna: no one takes the idea of sublimation seriously, as a biological process, that is. And I realize it's hard to imagine if you don't live through it. How many times have I watched pictures of the hydrogen bomb exploding over Hiroshima? Imagining the horror is impossible—unless you lived it. It's the same for Kundalini: how to communicate its otherworldly aspects in simple, everyday language.

I can piece together only the merest fragment of a future from books. As a consequence of the backward-flowing method, some incredible something has taken possession of my entire being. I may struggle with it for the rest of my life, but that's fine with me. I'm not looking for a feel-good consciousness; I'm looking for the real thing. When I started to notice the things happening inside me, I knew the signs were real. I'd hoped for the real thing and I got it, more, perhaps, than I bargained for. *How do I integrate my life around it?*

What do I do with my life? How do I live it? What do I eat? How do I conduct myself? How do I deal with people? How do I make amends for past fuck-ups?

I feel a general alienation from people and realize that it's because I now live between two worlds: the world of the Kundalini that is rebuilding my being and the exterior world, which, before I went to St. Jean, was hardly my oyster. At least I'm not alone: in *Kundalini: The Evolutionary Energy in Man*, Gopi Krishna describes his pain at stumbling upon one of the side-effects: "My love for them (humanity) seemed to be dead beyond recall."[28]

Although my diet is stable, the fact that I can eat anything leads me to consume more than I need. A former vegetarian, I am no longer attracted to that diet. Perhaps it's because, as a vegetarian, I was always tempted by other foods, eventually slipping back to meat. There must be something specific for my condition and although I try many variations, for the most part keeping my appetite under control, I do not find it. I feel unsatisfied, as if my diet ought to be more enabling of my transformation. After all, next to the Prana, which drives the process, food and drink are the only substances I ingest.

At the beginning, Gopi Krishna suffered even more, until the moment he hit on the idea of frequent short snacks of high quality organic foods. The idea appeared to him, as if, in his own words "suggested by an invisible intelligence."[29]

• • •

When I move onto Roper's house in Virginia, the first thing I do is throw away the double-knit shirts and pants, official closure with my father, for the moment.

While staying with Roper, it hits me. I'll go to India via France. I want to encounter a primary source, someone who can shed light on, reveal, interpret, or otherwise clarify my situation. To hear: 'Oh, the backward-flowing method, of course. Sure, I know all about it. Now, here's what you have to do…'

I guess it's the desire to compare my experience with that of others—all part of readjusting to the 'real world.' I expect to travel to Kashmir to meet Gopi Krishna—that is the goal. Planning a step-by-step course of action during the hectic first months after St. Jean—well, after being alone for so long, I'm vulnerable to the spiritual hype sweeping the western world. I have trouble focusing. First, the abortive mad-scramble to get back to my father. Then having to get away from him.

Mornings and evenings are spent with Roper and his wife, Juanita, in extreme Yoga sessions. He's latched on to Yoga and is going at it with all the intensity of a leveraged buyout. I do my one-hour then read until they finish standing on their heads for another thirty minutes. Roper is more of a Yoga fanatic than I've ever been. They are stoned before they start and remain stoned until they crash at night. At any moment, day or night, Roper jumps up and shouts, "Let's do Yoga!" And off they head to the workout room, mumbling about my lack of commitment.

When I try to talk to them about my experience, their eyes glaze over and they go to the refrigerator to warm up the cold roast beef. They like exertion—the physical pleasure attached to Hatha Yoga. The stillness of meditation seems like a backward step. I try to not betray any sign of judgment.

I take a gig helping Juanita with her gardening business. The sturdy Juanita and I work hard: cutting, pruning, cultivating and raking her customers' landscapes. I am amazed at my energy. Juanita is an inspiration. The heavier the loads she shoulders, the more inspired I am to follow.

Soon I have money for India. I'm counting on finding people, a colony—loose or otherwise—of highly evolved people. Watching Roper and Juanita almost makes me afraid of Yoga, as if they are out to kill themselves as surely as my father with his smokes.

My last night in Virginia, we go to a Mexican restaurant in Seven Corners. Bringing the check, the waiter asks, "Is everything okay?"

"Who made this?" asks Roper.

"Made what, sir?"

"This salsa."

"They use a power mower to chop it?" asks Juanita.

With that, the waiter's afraid to ask us to pay up, so we sit there talking.

"You believe that meditation develops special powers, don't you?" asks Juanita.

"That's a loaded question. Let's just say it's capable of expanding consciousness."

"No special, groovy powers?" asks Juanita.

"That you can demonstrate?" asks Roper.

The conversation makes me uncomfortable. It's always the same. I tell them: "There's nothing anecdotal about it. It's not like sports trivia."

"You mean it's reserved for the elite?" asks Roper.

I chuckle. "Sadly, you may be right. It doesn't work unless you're dedicated. That's the elite part. The elite are the dedicated."

"How do you become dedicated then?" asks Juanita.

"That's the Catch-22," I say.

"What do you mean?" asks Roper.

"Look, anything I say you'll think I'm going overboard and you'll pull back. If you really want it, you'll find it."

On the way back to the house, Roper throws out the idea of us all going to India. Juanita jumps all over it.

"It'll be fun. We can get some of those Indian carpets and study Yoga with a master. And you can find yourself a true guru," she says.

Hey, I'm not on a shopping spree.

"Uh, oh. He's got that look, babe," says Roper.

"Tell you what," I say, waxing reckless. "Let the book decide. If the *I Ching*'s for it, we'll go."

"Oh, the *I Ching*," says Juanita. "I love the *I Ching*. You've got to show me how to do it."

Back home, I copy out my table of numerological equivalencies for Juanita. Then she throws the coins.

 41. SUN / Decrease

Decrease does not under all circumstances mean something bad.

Six in the third place means:
When three people travel together,
Their number decreases by one.
When one man journeys alone,
He finds a companion.

"Well, I guess that's that," says Roper.

"Guess so," I sigh, tremendously relieved.

"Funny why they throw coins," says Juanita. "Why don't they just open the book to any old page and go from there?"

"It has to do with luck and probability," says Roper. "And once you open a book to a page, it tends to open again at that same page."

"Why?" asks Juanita.

"Creases in the binding. Brother, I don't know. Shit. Who wants to do Yoga?"

12—Consolidation

Master Lü-Tsu said, When there is a gradual success in producing the circulation of the light, a man must not give up his ordinary occupation in doing so. The ancients said, When occupations come to us, we must accept them; when things come to us, we must understand them from the ground up.[30]

> ~ *The Secret of the Golden Flower*—Lu Yen - Richard Wilhelm, Translator

It was hectic, the day I met Martine. Days are always hectic when you have to drive deep into the Paris suburbs.

I have ventured forth in my newly purchased *Quatrelle* to witness the departure of Swami Muktananda. I'm not keen on the shotgun approach to finding a teacher, especially a sensation like Muktananda, surrounded, as it were, by layers of handlers who seem little more than glorified bouncers. Anyway, someone told me about him. So I thought—what the hell.

To enter the ashram, I have to stand in line and be screened. Waiting to enter the big room, I overhear his acolytes buzzing about who is going to ride with him in the car to the airport. That is the spiritual concern of the day. More like backroom political maneuvering—jockeying for votes, bargaining for influence.

And the prize? Proximity to the guru during the final trip to Charles de Gaulle Airport. The winners get to ride; the losers get to follow in a motorcade. Dressed in robes of saffron, white and red, they huddle by the door whispering and cajoling, earnestly vying to move up the ladder of distinction.

Attended by still more acolytes who buzz around him, the guru is seated on a platform in the big room. I watch him while the bouncers quiz me. I picture Milarepa alone in his Himalayan cave. Somehow, the two don't jibe.

I have a vague idea about the questions I want to ask, but when I'm finally admitted to the big room, I see it may be impossible. First, I am one of a large group of people seated on the floor. I may never be recognized to speak because of the on-going ritual. All this makes me impatient, for I am only interested in knowing if the illustrious guru has some answers to my specific condition. The ceremony, trappings and schmoozing make me uncomfortable. I'm sorry that I've driven through all that Parisian traffic. And now I have to sit through the chanting, which I guess would have its place if the context didn't resemble a White House press conference with its hubbub of kibitzers and white noise.

If any present are on a spiritual mission, personal or otherwise, I can't detect it. It seems more like the worship of a particular personality, whose followers take their status from proximity to the Master.

I am probably missing the true meaning of the chanting, but the shuffling, the ritual mutterings of Muktananda, only underline the general impatience, as if everyone in the room is waiting for the mad scramble to the cars.

I can't remember if he asks for questions, I just remember my hand being in the air at a particular moment and his pointing at me. The noise level drops to zero as I stammer forth. Can't remember my exact words, only a paraphrase: "I recently spent one year in isolation, meditating. During this time hidden channels in my body were awakened…and eventually energy streamed into a place…a location in my head…that I can only call the third eye. Now, it continues on its own without my intervention, and my head cracks while it does…"

The Guru interrupts me. His acolytes turn their faces expectantly, as if ready to savor his reaction. My fellow floor sitters turn to stare at me.

"It is not possible. The head does not crack. There are no muscles in the head…" replies Muktananda.

Giggles and titters, as if the crowd were saying, "You don't know that, stupid? Everyone knows that!"

"Then something is cracking in every room I've occupied…"

"It wasn't your head."

"It must have been the radiators then," says someone in the crowd.

More derisive laughter. I'm not so much annoyed by people laughing at me as by the complete refusal to accept the possibility of a head cracking. That's what growth is all about, from infancy to maturity—the head changing imperceptibly over time.

"That is impossible; the skull cannot crack," he continues.

"But can it change its shape?"

"That is another matter."

He whispers to someone behind him in a light green robe. Everybody rises. Question time is over.

In his denial, is he saying that it didn't happen to him so therefore it couldn't happen…period? I don't put any limits on the power inside me. Obviously, once maturity is reached, cracking might be difficult, but not impossible. Being him, I would have wanted to hear more. Being me, I believed he could look at me and see my inner workings, and therefore know I was telling the truth.

So, I am disappointed, but not much. It only reinforces what I've learned. I figure I need a few experiences like this to learn to ignore conventional wisdom. In the solitude of St. Jean, as a kind of empirical detective, I learned to keep my mouth shut, perhaps by virtue of having no one to talk to. And now, reintroduced into the world, I am flush with success, like I have accomplished something—even though, in my heart of hearts, I know I haven't. The road is never ending—for as long as I have the strength to push my body out of bed. It's the same for the ordinary person as it is for the enlightened.

Good for you, I say to myself while walking into the bistro across the street from the ashram. You got laughed at and you deserved it. Now wake up, continue on your way, and forget conventional wisdom—even from the mouths of the so-called enlightened.

I sit at a table under a length-of-the-room mirror and order a *Carrotte Rapé* and a grilled Turbot with rice. That's when I catch sight of Martine. By that I mean, recognize her from the ashram. Plus, she is looking me over with let's-get-connected eyes. So we get connected. I ask her over.

"What did you think of it?" she asks.

"I dunno." I hold back, figuring she has an angle. I want to hear her take first.

"I thought he was awfully rude," she says.

Martine is French—soft red hair, inquisitive eyes.

"Your English…very good," I say. "I thought you guys didn't go in for this spiritual stuff—like us Americans—we're suckers for it."

"Actually, I'm doing research."

"Newspaper or university?" I ask.

"An article, separating the phonies from the real achievers."

"How do you tell the difference?"

"Maybe it sounds irrational, but I go on gut-feel. That's why I wanted to meet you. I felt you had a lot more to say and he just shut you up."

Two hours later, Martine is enjoying her third *café expres* and we are winding down.

"How did you get into this in the first place?" she asks.

"It probably sounds strange, but a part of my childhood was lost. I went looking for it and this is where I ended up."

"You mean you started meditating to remember the past?"

"In a way."

"Did you find it?"

"Yes, and no. I had an accident. Certain abilities disappeared all of a sudden…music being one of them…math another. It was a sign."

"A sign?"

"Yes, a sign that my body was imploding."

"You mean going back in time?"

"No, changing, deforming, at variance with my intended physical structure. I believe a blueprint of our bodies exists before our conception. What we do during life can impact how our actual body conforms to the blueprint."

"And you can prove this?"

"I never thought about it, but yes, I believe I can…eventually. My implosion had to do with nerve blockage."

Martine is persistent. She insists that we go to her place to continue. She is overjoyed with a Paris-by-night car trip in the *Quatrelle*, at not having to wait for the last Metro. I drive to her apartment on the rue Nicholas Charlet at the edge of Montparnasse, nudge the car into a small spot, and, once in her apartment, feel like crashing. Martine is full of energy, but finally takes pity on me. There is only one bed. She insists that we share it.

I've been out for over eight hours, so I still have my last meditation of the day. I lie still in the bed and close my eyes. Without really being asleep, I am soon transported into the ethereal world where I form a picture, a vision of cables and pulleys in an elevator shaft. Only there are two elevator cars with two sets of cables. While the cars rise and descend, the trick is to keep them at the same height. That is the work of the pulleys—to let out and take in slack. I realize that the cars are my lungs. The pulleys and cables are the channels between the control mechanism—the third eye.

I wake from my dream state, my head pinging as my shoulders circle in swift and violent involuntary motions. I feel Martine watching me writhe in her bed. What is she thinking? I soon find out.

Down below the sheets, she is kissing me. I am with someone who wants to share my experience, but can't…so she turns to sex, as if the joining of our physical bodies can somehow make a permanent connection between our astral bodies.

Feeling her lips stops the involuntary movements. I pull her to me and kiss her. I explain that, since my transformation, ejaculation has an adverse effect. She says she understands, then asks me if I've had sex recently. No. Plus, I am ten times more sensitive to touch than before. If I can't make love, would I lick her instead?

For a moment I can't answer, but realize that the inevitable has arrived because I'm too stimulated to refuse. "I can't risk ejaculating…My head will implode and I don't know if I can manufacture enough elixir to offset the ill effects."

Nevertheless, after more kissing, she pushes my head down below the sheets and spreads her legs. The more I lick, the more she likes it, the more it turns me on, the closer I am to coming. To hold back, I lock my scrotum. But it's painful, holding back. I'm not used to it. And she is moving so violently I finally have to release myself. I come all over the sheets the moment she starts to throb.

I lie there exhausted, my head aching. Martine strokes me, telling me that although she understands, it's been a long time for her, too. How many times have I heard that from a woman, who shortly after, confesses she's been with some guy three times a day for the last six years? Anyway, as I doze, she continues on about my experience, how unique it is, how she understands what I am going through.

But she doesn't. How could she? My head is imploding and the elixir is being summoned to my brain for life support. I curl up in a fetal position. To no avail, my nerves are like an electrical fire searing the very conduits that enclose them and there isn't enough elixir to cool them.

I sit up, unable to slip from dozing into sleep. I am wide awake. Certainly, if I try to lead a normal sex life, I'll simply exhaust my resources. Every factory runs on power; this one manufactures its own. And the conduits, which convey the energy to the replenishment points, are burning up. For one thing, they need nourishment. I can feel the elixir waning and, as Gopi Krishna put it, 'a tongue of golden flame searching my stomach for food.'[31]

"Are you okay?" asks Martine.

"You think I'm a freak."

"No, I don't."

"Do you have any yogurt?"

"I think so…in the fridge."

Naked, I stumble to the fridge and grab a Yoplait. Four containers later, I feel somewhat calmed. Martine comes into the kitchen and stands by me, softly massaging my shoulders.

"How do you feel?" she asks.

"Better."

"Do you think you can sleep?"

Back in bed together, after another episode of involuntary movements, Martine gets to witness the ultimate in CPR. I say it only figuratively, for how can she see the muscle walls of my solar plexus open and the Pranic energy stream forth enroute to the third eye? Yet, as we lie there, I sense her watching me, wondering if I am in the grip of some sort of fit. Nevertheless, she is fascinated, as if hoping to catch a glimpse of the power that is tossing me around her bed.

• • •

I am awake before Martine, not knowing if the daylight will frame me as an intriguing, yet inconsequential one-night stand. I don't know if she is truly interested in my experience, or merely a spiritual groupie. After a year in isolation, I am like a Wildman suddenly turned loose on the world. What's more, I haven't come back to the world empty-handed. I have a mission, and there's no greater turn-off to friends and acquaintances than a man on a mission.

So, how to get on with my self-imposed mission? I describe it thusly because everyone who has an experience like mine is hounded by the obligation to communicate the wonder of it. Ideas like *advancing the cause of consciousness in a consciousness-challenged world* keep gnawing at me.

But I am reticent. New phenomena occur every day. At the beginning, the magic elixir and the healing wind, later involuntary movements. Now all of a sudden, I've stopped dreaming. I'm at a loss about how to communicate an experience that keeps changing. Perhaps, it will just stop, although I doubt it. Martine says I should write a book. In *Kundalini: The Evolutionary Energy in Man*, Gopi Krishna tells of "hesitating twenty years in making my experience public because in the first place, I wanted to make myself completely sure about my condition, and secondly, I was entirely averse to exposing myself to the criticism of well-meaning friends and the ridicule of opponents."[32]

His declaration confirms the unpredictable nature of Kundalini. It doesn't stand still. By the time I think I understand what's happening, something new is occurring. That's why I don't rush out and proclaim it to the world, only to see the whole thing evaporate. But when sex is the driving force behind Kundalini and at the same time, behind a male-female relationship, a normal life is difficult. I am being pulled in two directions—toward a reconciliation with the 'real' world and, at the same time, under the sway of Kundalini. Somehow, I must straddle them both. I am not brave enough to walk away from Martine, especially after such extended loneliness.

From the outset there are problems, because my vigor has to be shared for both spiritual and temporal needs. No beating around the bush—once you awaken Kundalini, you have to come to terms with its effect on your sex life. The irony is: I am more vigorous than before, and just as attracted by women. But self-protection is a stronger instinct. A higher purpose has requisitioned my vital energy. I am forced to give precedence to the Kundalini. I don't have a choice. Once awakened, the Kundalini doesn't stop or go on vacation. And as the intervals between our intercourse lengthen, I know that I am being unfair to Martine, but every time I ejaculate, it's *Sturm und Drang*. My head literally implodes and I have to lie in bed shaking and shivering. It takes me two full recovery days to restore my energies.

I remember reading that sex has two purposes:

• Replenishing the race, and
• Furthering consciousness (sublimation).

Hell, nowadays, ordinary people think of sex in terms of performance, the sex act on a scale of 1 to 10. Like some new Olympic
event. The notion becomes self-defining. Where does it originate?
Left to its own devices, the mind conjures up amazing feats of prowess, which it uses to embellish the self-myth. It's addictive. And like
most addictions, it's culturally manufactured. The imagination sucks
up the cultural white noise: *what an appetite...the world's greatest
cocksman...a 10 all the way...horny till he was 80...ten women in
a three-hour period...a hunk...the HOTTEST guy around...lusty...
potent...virile.*

I look back on my record of addictions: cigarettes—I barely
remember them; alcohol—a distant memory; drugs—they dropped
away of their own accord; sex. Except for occasional problems in our
relationship, I have no regrets; I'm at peace with my sexuality. As for
the outside world, sex goes way beyond replenishing the race.

Martine is shy and loath to bring up the subject. Yet, it's a
stumbling block, albeit unspoken, for the most part. When it does
come up, I find us repeating the same words over and over.

"I want you to come in me," she says one night. "I love it when
you do."

"I have to hold back," I say.

"But you never take any pleasure for yourself."

"I take pleasure from giving you pleasure...plus, it hurts to
ejaculate."

"Hurts?" she murmurs.

"Debilitates me."

"Oh."

"Just touching you gives me intense pleasure. Sex is like walking on the razor's edge. It's the number one pleasure, the number one
destroyer."

"You don't like it?"

"You don't understand what I'm saying, do you?"

"I'm trying to."

"One day, I may have to stop altogether."

"I don't like it when you say that, darling."

"Sublimation is real," I say. "You see this side of my chest?
It's more pronounced, more developed than the other." I point at a

bone. "This bone appeared about a year and a half ago. The causal body is the blueprint for the physical body; it precedes it. If the physical body is deformed…by whatever means…Kundalini wants to enlarge it to the size and shape of the ideal causal body. Suppose I had arthritis. When the third eye assumes control, it starts to rebuild the physical body using the blueprint of *the* perfect body, which has existed since my unique bodily substantiation was conceived. It would attack my arthritis. It wipes away all deformities. First and foremost, it's a healing force."

"That's the passion, the fanaticism, I was talking about," she says, collapsing on the bed. "You see, it's so clear to you."

"Because I lived it. I was a very good singer as a kid. The accident deformed me. My deformity is the reason I can no longer sing or play music."

"Write it down. Make it clear. Show them how to put the third eye back in charge…by revealing the backward-flowing method to the world. And while you're at it, maybe you can talk about the healing aspect…instead of consciousness. Other writers have beaten that one to death. Healing is urgent."

"You amaze me," I say.

"I've got to dress."

"You don't want to meditate?"

"Maybe later. I have to go to the office…in the meantime, give me your journal to read in the Metro."

That is another stumbling block. Martine is a dabbler. She likes listening to supernatural tales the way some people enjoy supermarket weeklies. But that's as far as it goes. She attends Yoga class, but doesn't like practicing at home with me. Yet neither sex nor Yoga sabotages our relationship. As the months fly by, routine habit, as much as anything else, holds us together in mutual co-dependency. I'd like to think that I've evolved sufficiently not to need a woman. In fact, I'd like to announce that I am packing up and moving to a cave in the Himalayas—just like Milarepa. My condition has me believing I ought to. And I want to live up to the nobility of it, not down to the level of the world around me. Living in the real world, however, means doing real world things, like forgetting where I parked the car or arguing with Martine about writing. Anyway, I'm not ready for adventure; the Kundalini has me tethered to the civilized world where I can oversee my rehabilitation in relative comfort. Every time Martine suggests taking a trip, I tell her I don't dare leave Paris.

• • •

"I have a job for you," she says one day. "You can start when we come back from India, if you want it."

"I don't know about India, Martine. Besides, I've already found a job. I was going to tell you later, after dinner."

"That's great. What is it?" she asks.

"Lionel wants me to paint his apartment. You know, I don't know if I can handle spicy Indian food now."

"They have western-style restaurants."

"All over?"

"Of course," says Martine. "Painting Lionel's place? It's huge. How much is he paying?"

"Three thousand francs."

"Not bad, but it'll take a long time, *n'est-ce pas?*"

"About one month. So what's your job?"

"Eric, who works at the paper..."

"I remember Eric."

"Well, Eric is looking for an American that can give English lessons and translate French documents into English. It would mean teaching a class. I told him about you."

"I'm de man...and...maybe I can whack out Lionel's apartment at night. He's really anxious," I say. "You really think I could survive in India with all that spicy food?"

"Don't you want to meet Gopi Krishna?" she asks.

"I thought you didn't want to go to Kashmir."

"Kashmir is on the way to Ladakh and I want to go to Ladakh."

"Two birds with one stone, *alors*...except...don't they have a revolution going on?"

"Not really, just a military buildup."

13—India

The first reality we come across is consciousness. The world comes later. We know first ourselves and then the world. So the wiser course is first to understand the knower. What modern thinkers have done is to ignore or bypass the knower, forgetting that it is the knower that is doing it.

~ *The Awakening of Kundalini*—Gopi Krishna

artine and I land in Shrinagar on a hop from New Delhi. The little airport doesn't have much throughput and most of that is official Indian military business. The full-scale Muslim rebellion in Kashmir has not yet broken out; nevertheless the airport is surrounded by fortified emplacements. Soldiers with machine guns and half-tracks are everywhere in August of 1977. Not only is the Muslim threat a constant worry, Shrinagar is also the jumping-off place for the Indian defense of Ladakh, the Himalayan province inhabited by Tibetan peoples. Since China seized control of Tibet in the '50s and fought a couple of border wars with India, the Indian defense establishment uses Shrinagar as its logistical HQ for maintaining their defensive outposts high in the Himalayas.

Once cleared through immigration, the guides swarm over us. One persistent little gentleman catches Martine's fancy. It's almost as if he's decided that we are entrusted to him, that he will guide and shelter us. Not pushy or obvious like the others, Farad greets us politely then holds back while the others bombard us with pleas and enticements in English peppered with Urdu.

Martine has researched the town, and we probably would have ended up in one of the hotels, but Farad politely explains that he has something more suitable. Something about a lake. We huddle; I don't want to be the one to give the okay and then have Martine not like it. Farad's polite English and patient approach convinces her and he loads our stuff into a taxi. Soon after, we arrive at Dal Lake.

The houses on the mountains overlooking Dal Lake are constructed with bare wooden and brick siding, which gives them a kind of mixed Norman/Alpine appearance if it wasn't for the fact that the various floors resemble slices from completely different houses stacked one upon the other. Each floor has its own architectural eccentricities: overhanging porches; arched windows on one floor, rectangular on the next; rounded corners, straight corners; painted and unpainted trim. The effect is somehow symmetrical even though the various parts seem to be inspired by altogether different architectural styles.

Surrounded by the mountains, the lake itself, a surface of over ten square miles, is home to an array of houseboats ranging from simple to splendidiforous. Water-borne merchants in *shikaras*[33] float by on a bed of lotus petals as Sampan cooks dump garbage into the black waters.

Most tourists live better in the ornate houseboats for their two-week vacations than they do at home. Farad's houseboat—that we learn is a boat only after we arrive in the *shikara* water taxi—is somewhere in the mid-range. Farad explains that his father was in the British Army and the Raj tradition of service and courtesy is in his blood. Farad doesn't have a wife; nevertheless everything is taken care of. He prepares the meals; elaborate stews containing fresh vegetables and exotic spices, one of which resembles a furry horse chestnut. He conducts us by boat or taxi wherever we want to go, and if we don't know where to go, he suggests something. He selects the sites for us to see, and he arranges my visit with Gopi Krishna.

It takes a week to locate him. All I have is: *Gopi Krishna, Shrinagar*. Not much to go on in a city of 700,000. But I give one of his books to Farad, and a couple of days later his cousin rows up to the boat with some good news. Through the grapevine, Farad has made contact with Gopi Krishna and his entourage, and an appointment is arranged. It is decided that Martine will hang out in the Nishat Bagh (the Gardens of Gladness) while I meet with Gopi Krishna.

I don't know what to expect, haven't thought about it really. I only know that I don't prepare. The premeditated business call is foreign to me. Like most encounters, I wing it. But heck, I'll meet him and what happens, happens. And that is a bone of contention between us. Martine wants me to make lists, take notes, even pictures. Maybe I should have. Yet, to this day I recall our conversation. It wasn't complicated or esoteric.

For that, I'm grateful. No pretensions. He doesn't run a lot of spiritual smack, he just gets down to business with a kind of Great Gildersleeve drawling, "Yesssss?" Throws me back, it does. I immediately picture Martine with a ready smile and a million variants on a dozen themes. She would have handled it, but now I have to bounce back even though his one-word interrogatory deflates me.

I have the feeling that he's been expecting me. I don't know why. No one knows we are here. It was set up at the last minute, but he's acting guardedly, as if testing me. Why? I wonder. For authenticity? How can that be measured or verified? Can the adept see past the onionskin of the physical body into the causal?

I stammer forth, summarizing my Kundalini experience, hoping this thing we hold in common will make him less perfunctory. To a degree that happens, but rather than conversing, he mostly gives me a checklist for contending with Kundalini.

He tells me that it may never end, that it is rebuilding my body to some sort of perfect state.

"It may take years," he says. "Each person's experience is different."

"I don't think it's temporary," I say.

"No. Yours is one of the most far-reaching, permanent Kundalini awakenings I've encountered. Rare, very rare indeed. There are a few things you must know."

"Oh?"

"First, don't travel."

"If that's number one, I guess coming to India on a Russian charter and getting thrown into a holding pen in Kiev for six hours without a bathroom, then walking the streets of New Delhi in the summer heat was not the proper way to observe the first commandment. But that's nothing, we're on our way to Ladakh."

"Ladakh? That's a three-day bus trip over the Himalayas. A very difficult, dangerous trip!"

"My wife wants to go there."

"You're married?"

"Un-huh."

"Then you must know about number two. No sex."

"I never ejaculate. It drains the energy out of my head. I feel like I'm imploding."

"For now, the energy must not flow out. When the process has finished, you can have a better-than-normal sex life."

"I may live so long." He looks at me queerly. "That's a Jewish expression," I say.

"Are you Jewish?" he asks, a bit confused as to why I brought it up.

"No."

"Have you been sick?"

"I get bronchitis, and colds that last longer than usual. It may be the damp Paris climate."

"Your whole somatic and nervous systems…" he says.

"I never take medicine, just sweat it out with natural remedies."

"That will improve until you are no longer even ill. Your diet…"

"Organic, natural foods."

"It's okay to eat meat," he says. "You may need it, but this will change and someday you may not need meat. You'll know when."

"France has plenty of fresh markets and natural foods. At first, I took frequent, small meals: yogurt, toast, milk, honey. Tea, no coffee. Just before the awakening I was eating a few spoonfuls of yogurt and couple of sesame seeds a day. Yet I had too much energy."

"How are you at coping with the stress of work?"

"I'm lucky. My job is teaching *me* to interact with people. The only thing is…"

"Yes?"

"Sometimes I lose control. Not with my students, with the office politics. The French, you know. It's not something new. As a child I was emotionally volatile. When the Kundalini happened, I thought I'd been reborn psychologically."

He stands up, comes closer, and faces me directly. "You were petulant as a child, now you are changing."

"Do people change?"

"Look in the mirror. Is your body changing?"

"Yes."

"So?"

"Yes, I remember how my personality changed as my appearance changed…after my childhood accident."

"You are changing again. Now make something of it."

"The problem is I can't figure out what to do."

"Writing about it helped me. I waited a long time before starting. Does it matter if it's three years or thirty?"

"Well, in the West the idea of achievement hangs over our lives from birth."

I take an extended look around the room. The house seems to be on the grounds of a large estate, but I don't ask. The room itself is spare and his bright white Pandit robes give off a phosphorescent luster in the afternoon light. For a man born in 1903, he appears strong, erect and powerful.

"You live in the city," he continues. "Walks in the country are what you need for this work."

"You call it work, too?"

"All consuming work. The nerves need to be revitalized…every nerve in your body…and while that's being done, the muscles, the sinews. Until your body is perfect, and that takes time. Long walks in the country off the beaten path…away from people."

"That's what I crave. It isn't possible yet. But we've talked about buying a house in the country."

"Has it stopped—the Kundalini—has it stopped even once?" he asks.

"It's there 24 hours a day. Fortunately, I have your books. When it happened, I had nothing except my wits."

I stand up, prepare to leave.

"Don't look for a teacher," he says. "A teacher is only as effective as his authenticity. In this work, authenticity means empirical knowledge. You have men with great charisma, but little authenticity."

"I went to see Swami Muktananda," I say. "He told me that my head couldn't crack…well, I meant to say *change shape*, but said *crack* instead, because that's what it feels like. Anyway, he didn't agree."

"No one will, so *you* be the authority," he says, nodding his head. "Got it?"

Me, an authority? I don't quite understand, so I blurt out the first thing that pops into my mind. "I guess people ask you about God all the time."

"Yes. But for you, learning what to eat and how to live with Kundalini is crucial. Don't listen to people's opinions. Learn as much as possible about your true nature, about your body. These secret functions of the body are part of a science, you know. An ancient one, but still valid."

• • •

The taxi is waiting for me on the dirt road. When I reach it, I look back at the house on the hill. Gopi Krishna emerges, follows a path to another door where he meets a woman. His posture and bearing betray no sign of age or weakness. I climb into the taxi as they stand there conversing.

On the way to the gardens, I think about adding to the catalog of esoteric literature. For some reason, it doesn't feel right, even with Martine constantly prodding me. I have something to say and I have support. So what's holding me back?

The gardens are empty. I find Martine drinking tea with the caretaker outside his little house. He offers me a cup. I sit down, smile, and ask her about the garden. After the tea, we take a spin around while Martine debriefs me.

"Well?" she begins. I am getting tired of the businesslike approach.

"Short and sweet," I reply.

"What do you mean?"

"No spiritual double-talk."

Martine tilts her head. I can see that she is disappointed. Guess I'm not a very good interviewer.

"That's how it went," I say. "Matter-of-factly. Completely the opposite of the Muk."

"Did he see you?" she asks.

I peer over at her. "You mean into me?"

"Yes."

"I don't know. I often ask myself that question. Is there any person, or machine, that can detect Kundalini activity inside a living being?"

"I've been reading his Kundalini book," says Martine. "Funny, I never read him before, don't know why."

"He only appeals to highly intelligent people," I say.

"Ha-ha. Listen to this: 'How many have published their spiritual experiences to afford a glimpse of the transcendental to other seekers in order to inspire them and to provide guidance on the path? In India, the number of enlightened during the last one hundred years can be counted on the fingers of one hand. The famous seers of the Upanishads—and even Buddha—had to adduce proofs for the authenticity of their own experiences'[34]. How does anyone figure this stuff out?"

"Gopi Krishna's great accomplishment is the clarification of his empirical discoveries. His taking a scientific, rather than a religious approach."

"And what about you? Sometimes I don't know how you put up with being a walking experiment."

"It's the Scot's blood in me."

"So what did he say?" asks Martine.

"He gave me a checklist—Like in the *Secret of the Golden Flower: A Magic Spell for the Far Journey*. I have it here in my notebook; I wrote it down in the taxi: eat good, natural food, no sex until it stabilizes—we've been there once or twice, plenty of sleep and rest, don't get sick because it'll be much worse than for a normal person, avoid stress in the workplace, take plenty of walks in the country, don't look for a teacher, oh, and one more, don't travel—so I shouldn't be here and definitely am not going to Ladakh."

"Well, I've got a message for Mr. Krishna," says Martine. "I'm going to Ladakh; I want to see Tibet. Did he tell you where you could go? Or do you want me to?"

Back in the taxi, Martine continues. "He wasn't curious about you? Maybe he's working with somebody else."

I shake my head. "I wouldn't read anything into it. He's seventy-four years old."

"Well, who needs Gopi Krishna when you have me," she says, cuddling up to me in the taxi.

"All the way to Ladakh and back…on the bus."

• • •

I don't know why I confessed my emotional volatility to Gopi Krishna, yet looking back, that's what I did—asked him for advice. Well, no harm. But it's true; I have a problem. And though I don't normally talk about it, I've always been impatient with indecisive people. But hey, that's the first thing that struck me about Gopi

Krishna—the way he greeted me impatiently. I pictured myself in his place, ready to dismiss *me* if I turned out to be a dabbler. Perhaps, that's why our conversation got more discerning as it progressed. Perhaps, it's only impatient types like Gopi Krishna and myself who succeed in this *work*. Resilient, defiant people. People, who fail miserably early on, yet refuse to stay down.

I don't know if I'm reading too much into it after spending only forty minutes with him. In any case, I can't talk to Martine about it, these are my very private thoughts. She thinks I'm holding back. Not holding back actually, just unable to share the unshareable, I tell her. But whether I'm right about the type of personality that succeeds on *The Far Journey*, I know over time I will absorb everything he said. That's the way my mind functions. Sometimes I can *leap over and penetrate directly*; other times, it takes a while.

For some reason, Martine is edgy. I guess I should know why, but I don't. Is it because of Gopi Krishna or because I'm not looking forward to Ladakh?

• • •

The buses in Muslim countries are a trip. Heaped with chickens in wooden cages, suitcases secured with extra ties against the wind, lumpy sacks of sundries about to explode, and finally a goat or two, they huff and puff across the countryside. Donkeys, carts, mopeds, pedestrians and night drivers without lights—anything and everything rolls by outside. And the same objects that ride on top of buses also ride inside, paired up, as it were, with their owners. And their owners—mostly male—chain-smoke some noxious form of black tobacco.

Our bus is no different. First, there are no women, so everyone, apart from Martine and myself, smokes heavily-scented black tobacco. Second, if you understand Urdu, you'll feel at ease on the three-day trek over the Himalayas. I'm sure that the speakers are regaling each other with heroic tales from great Pashtoon legends, but if you don't understand one word—not just words spoken calmly, but words shouted between seatmates at infinitesimal ranges—your nerves will gradually crack. The twisting mountain roads are demanding enough, never mind the Indian Army trucks that careen down the mountain in the other direction. Trucks, whose drivers enjoy lightening the boredom of ferrying infantry with a cloud-capped version of chicken, scaring our timid driver to death and necessitating a kind of defensive, roll-with-it approach, sending the passengers and livestock from one side of the bus to the other. Of course, the stopovers, where I get so badly bitten by bedbugs that my left eye closes up, occasioning the craning of heads and great Pashtoon giggles, are a bonus. Funny thing about bedbugs, they always prefer one member in a couple. And the favorite is always me. Whether it's the acid mantle of my skin that attracts them or skinniness of my frame, I have bites all over my body. I am swollen, exhausted, and irritable when we arrive. Gopi Krishna's travel warning has eaten a large area of my brain. If I survive, I resolve to stay put.

"Take trips by yourself," I say. "Leave me to my students."

I can see Martine reading into my words; I phrase them that way on purpose—to test her.

"It's a moot point, *chérie*," she says. "The house we're going to buy is going to take all our time over the next five years."

"Rather masonry and carpentry than bedbugs."

"And the book? You are going to do it now, aren't you?"

"I'm thinking about it."

"I thought you said Gopi Krishna advised you to."

"Well, he did mention it, and I do think about it, but..."

I can see it; Martine is disappointed. But the big thing now is sex. Because of my exhaustion, I haven't been able to perform on the trip. Fortunately, she is tired, too, and on the houseboat, with Farad on the other side of the bulkhead, it would have been like the beating drums of a slave ship.

Once in Ladakh, we relax. A primitive agricultural kingdom, Ladakh resembles the Shire of Hobbit fame—a Tibeto-Mongoloid version. The people are so relaxed we don't seem to bother their routine. Tourists walk among them, *oohing* and *ahhing* at the size of the yaks and the dribble-castle architecture of the temples.

Unlike Shrinagar where Farad refuses to let us go out unaccompanied, we get back to walking. Through the village of Leh, along the Indus River valley, into the hills and mountains. We eat and sleep well in our primitive hobbit castle guesthouse. Like the hobbit hutches, the rooms have rounded doorways, windows, and corners. I understand why hobbits like rounded corners; the bedroom is cozy and benign, giving off a special kind of vibe that occasions intimacy. For a week we settle for sex, and small talk with other tourists, steering clear of Martine's moodiness. But it's bound to pop out sooner or later.

14—Relapse

Groups don't think, act, or have motivations, only individuals do. Each individual is different from every other. How can we fit in one world? There isn't much in common when you extend the relationship beyond the one of mutual self-interest, so someone will have to sacrifice. Any relationship should last only as long as it is beneficial for each party. Intimacy needs to be cultivated and nourished.

~ *How I Found Freedom in an Unfree World*—Harry Browne

O ur new project has walls you can walk through and a living
room you have to row across when it rains. Martine and I
throw all our extra cash into it: replacing the dilapidated
slate roof, fashioning real walls out of crumbled ones, putting in
a floor where there is none. We watch the house become livable.
Whether it will ever be finished is another question. We decide to
compromise: forget the doodads and the chintz, and settle for a door
on a pair of sawhorses with barrels for stools. That's all the dining
table we'll need when Roper and Juanita visit us. We don't consider
setting up shop on the *rue Nicholas Charlet*; we aren't even going
to let them unpack. The odor of hawthorn, lilac and honeysuckle
beat the stench of the Metro any day. There's no reason to confine
Roper's nervous energy to a tiny Parisian apartment for more than a
couple of hours, all the time we'll need to load up the car and sail out
toward Normandy.

But first I have to settle at the office. I have my own school
now. Like any business owner, I can't afford to have things go wrong
while I'm away. So Martine drives to the airport while I trek down
to fine-tune the schedule. The haggling takes a while, but the result
is three uninterrupted weeks in the country followed by a return to
satisfied customers in September, I hope.

When I get home, Martine and Juanita emerge from the
kitchen with maps and charts. Roper is huffing and puffing around
our tiny apartment trying to avoid stepping all over our bed. He
blows by the ladies and without even a perfunctory greeting, sticks
his head in my face. "Have you crapped today, man?"

"...uh, no, I don't remember," I reply.

"That's what's wrong with you people. You don't shit by the
numbers. When was the last time you had a colonic?"

"Don't know what it is," I say.

"They stick a tube up your butt to flush out the colon,"
explains Martine.

"Brother, you're going to get one," says Roper. "I got the name
of a practitioner in Paris. This is going to change your..." He stops
suddenly, looks at me, as if seeing me for the first time.

"Look at that," he continues, pointing me out to Martine.

"We live at the 48th parallel, Roper. Ten months of the year there's no sun, and the two sunny months aren't necessarily July and August," I say.

"Well, I don't care if you're meditating and seeing the celestial feathers, you're getting a colonic when we get back. You want to live forever, don't you?"

Roper walks up close to me, sticks his face next to mine. Martine and Juanita stop what they were doing, mosey up alongside and stare with him. After a moment, Roper shakes his head and turns away.

"What is it?" asks Martine.

"I don't know yet. Not just the pale skin," he says.

"You haven't seen me in four years, Roper."

"What is it?" ask the women.

"Something about you's different," he says.

"I'm getting older."

"Not."

Martine and I disappear into the bedroom to pack. "I read your latest journal entry, the one about our meeting at the ashram…" she says, stuffing her suitcase, not paying attention to what goes in. She's usually so on top of things. But she's just filled her suitcase with ten sweaters? Maybe the country will relax her. I go over, pull the sweaters out one by one. Martine seems upset, almost angry with me.

Our *Quatrelle* has humped one load too many. To drive back and forth to Normandy, we've traded up to a *Renault 12 Break* (how the French get *Break* from *Station Wagon*, I'll never know). We need space for building materials. So, loaded up with lumber on top, bricks in the back, the four of us set out. As we drive through Versailles, Juanita holds forth on the tangled destinies of Napoleon and Josephine. To cap off our trip, I agree to have a colonic when we return. This puts Roper in the best of moods. I'm hoping he'll help me mix cement for the chimney.

Not only does he help, he throws his prodigious energies into the entire project. We work on the chimney, finishing it in four days. Follow that with the bedroom insulation project, which we finish in two. Finally, we dig a four-foot drainage ditch around the perimeter of the house. All this extra elbow grease leaves the mornings free. I stay upstairs writing in my journal until noon. Intermittently, Martine brings me tea and *tartines* with homemade black current jam. I can tell my note-taking impresses her, because she doesn't ask me about the book, as if my scribbling means I've made up my mind. But I haven't. I don't feel I can write a book on Kundalini until the whole thing is over, and perhaps, not even then.

"What did you do this morning?" I ask, hoping my small talk will drive her back to the kitchen so I can finish my entry.

"Oh, I took a walk with Juanita."

"Un-huh."

"Your friends are...nice."

"Oh?"

"A little unusual, but nice."

"I told you about Roper."

"Yeah, but I wasn't expecting to be asked if my shit floats."

"Does it?"

"As a matter of fact it does."

"You don't need a colonic then."

The last night, Roper drinks too much wine at dinner, becomes maudlin and corners me. "I know I'm a bit of a blowhard when I'm in my cups, but I'm going to miss you guys. I don't understand a thing you're doing. I don't get the school. You could be making a lot more money with me. And this house, it'll take you twenty years to finish. As far as meditation...I get lost in your 'Be Here Now' explanation."

At the other end of the table Martine and Juanita are discussing her son, Adam. As soon as Roper hears his stepson's name, he begins a running commentary.

"Adam...He's been fired from six jobs, always for the same thing. Fights with his boss. Won't listen. A sociopath...that's what he is."

"Sounds like a smart kid to me," I say.

"Yeah, if getting fired is smart...plus two failed marriages."

"Roper, people who don't get along with the boss are meant to work for themselves," I say.

"That's just it," says Roper. "It's okay to be a rebel if you have the talent to do your own thing."

"Alright, Roper, you don't like him," I whisper, pointing to Juanita, who's overheard Roper's comments.

"The hell with her. The hell with you, too. You're just like him."

And while he's talking, I'm thinking it's the perfect description of me. Just about every artist, writer, politician, inventor—every creative person alive—is a quasi-sociopath, who, if talented and strong enough to stand up to the world, become the ones who change it. But that's not me. I'm too addicted to my friends, as if they were surrogate parents or something. I still treasure the moments we've shared. Maybe that's why I can't write—because I don't want to offend anyone. I remember Martine telling me: "You have to write like everyone you know is dead."

"Loosen up on yourself, man," says Roper. "You made mistakes so you think you're a bad guy, but you're not. You're just uptight."

"Maybe you're right."

"So write that book, but don't make it too technical. Success isn't about expertise."

"What is it, then?" I ask.

"Charisma."

"Phonies can have charisma, as well saints and prophets."

"Saints and prophets are losers," says Roper. "You were a loser. You still act like one, but I know you're different now. How did you do it?"

"I gave up sex."

"You crazy fuck."

"That's how 'spiritual' transformation works. By diverting vital fluid into the nerves and up the spinal column."

"Jesus."

"You asked me about it once before, but you weren't serious."

"I'm not sure I'll ever be that kind of serious."

"Sublimation is abstinence with a higher purpose, Roper. The thing is, once you start, you can't go back."

"You crazy fucker."

"It's not like I'm impotent," I say. "I can get a hard-on, but ejaculating debilitates me."

"When I think of the ways I wasted it," says Roper, suddenly lost in thought. "I can't get a hard-on now. I feel like one of those fucked-out politicians. You can tell when a guy's fucked out."

"We're in the same boat, Roper."

"Nah, brother, you're using it for something. I'm just fucked out. I can't even have children."

When Roper realizes Juanita is staring at him, he changes the subject. Smiling and waving his glass at Martine, he shouts, "Don't ever do anything to piss her off, man. You don't want to lose her."

"By the way," asks Juanita, "how did you two meet?"

Martine gets up, starts puttering in the kitchen. *There's something about her movements that make me reluctant to launch into the standard narrative. Whatever I say will only make it worse—whatever it is.*

"You should read the description in his journal, very poetic," says Martine, as she scrubs at the dinner plates. "And, by the way, I didn't come to your table, you came to mine. But leave it as it is. It's good."

"One way or the other, what does it matter?" I ask. "If you care, I'll change it."

"But I don't care, *chérie*. I don't care," says Martine, slamming down the sponge.

By the time I stand up, Martine has fled to the bedroom. I get to the door as it slams in my face.

I look at Roper, then at Juanita. We sit down on a set of carved African stools, staring at our feet for what seems an eon.

"I don't suppose you know how to handle that, Roper," I say.

"It never bodes well," he says, looking at his wife. "That's for sure."

"I never know if it's something I did, or what," I say.

"Men never do," says Juanita.

"What's that supposed to mean, Babe?" asks Roper.

"Nothing, sweet pea, except you gotta do more than sit on a stool."

I stand up, intending to go to the bedroom.

Roper watches me. "Shit," he says, shouting in a loud, booming voice, "I know what's different."

His yelping brings Martine to the bedroom door.

"What is it?" she asks.

"His face is different. Like it's exploded outward." He swirls his hands in the air like he's tossing a pizza. "More rounded lines. And the shoulders. You're bigger. You stand out more."

Although there are smiles all around, I'm worried about Martine. It's as if she's feeling something before it's actually happened. And something tells me that when it does, it'll be one of my fuck-ups. And I'm wishing I could take the housing off my brain and bang the dents out to reshape my skull overnight. That's my real work and I can't even get to it until the Kundalini runs its course. And how long will that take? Sure, in the outside world I am succeeding: I have a wife, a successful business. I've come to terms with the world, sort of. And yet, my real work hasn't even begun, because the Kundalini proceeds according to its own inscrutable timetable. And whether I do more Yoga, take longer walks or exercise moderately or profusely, I can't speed up the process. Stillness is the only factor affecting my reconstruction.

Stillness, as in lying stock-still. That's when the Kundalini is productive. Add a daily dose of Yoga, just enough to keep the muscles and sinews toned, the shoulders, chest and arms worked out.

My life with Martine has defined an outer life of social meaning that provides the motivation for doing things, such as renovating the house and learning a profession. My main purpose has become secondary, usurped by the activity thrown up around our lives. At first, I welcome these activities as a break from the relentlessness of the Kundalini. Now, I rarely penetrate to the deepest level of stillness. In fact, I begin to doubt its validity. The oft-repeated phrases are a hollow echo in my head, like the pings and pops I feel when I lie down.

To pay my share of the bills, I have learned a profession. Martine and I have discussed the future, made plans, and restored a wretched house. We are like a small business suddenly fallen into bankruptcy. Fifteen years of frantic activity had taken my mind off my real work.

· · ·

Sophie, one of my partners, suggests we propose leadership conferences. Tells me a friend of hers just finished one. I get carried away by her enthusiasm and reveal just enough about my Kundalini experience to let her think she understands. She begs to hear more. Now, because of my loose lips, I have to put up with her constant probing. Remembering Gopi Krishna's words, I get that sinking feeling.

> "If I had done so much as even breathed to others a word about my abnormality and the bizarre manifestations which were now a regular feature of my life, I might have been labeled a lunatic and treated accordingly, meeting ridicule instead of compassion."[35]

And that was in India, a country with a supposed tolerance for spiritual pursuits.

Group Dynamics and Leadership, Sophie calls it. Says it'll be good for me to master the techniques if I ever want to instruct a group of students *'dans mon truc personnel'*[36].

"Group Leadership teaches you how to control a group," she says. "We could clone their *stage;*[37] later on, you could use it to fashion a spiritual workshop. You'd be surprised how much interest there is."

"What makes you think I'm interested in 'fashioning a spiritual workshop?'" I ask.

"Well, done the correct way, we can make a lot of money…as well as benefit a lot of people," she replies.

At that point, I figure, okay, I have to do it just to squelch the whole idea. So I sign up for the three days.

Group Dynamics and Leadership takes place in a large apartment on Boulevard Malesherbes. It's more of an 'encounter group' than a kind of formal pedagogy. Psychobabble from the 70s that's taken an extra decade to get to France. The first day's introductions are interesting enough—a group confessional, a chance for close-mouthed operatives to sit back and make the others feel uncomfortable about all their blabbing. The only memorable event—the one that helps me put the whole idea in perspective—is an afternoon exercise involving consensus.

'You're lost in a deep forest. It's getting dark. There are other people around you who could bring you out. What is the best way to locate them? One, stay put and let them find you. Two, shout in a high-pitched voice. Three, pitch your voices as low as possible and shout.'

We have 20 minutes to debate the subject and come to a decision. Like a jury, a minority verdict is unacceptable; it has to be a consensus, but making the right decision is equally important for it will save our lives. Having no prior knowledge of the subject, I listen for a few minutes as the other participants jump into animated debate. Headed by one very assertive, charismatic individual, the group seems to be moving toward the 'high-pitched' solution. Just when they are about to ask those of us who have not spoken if we agree, I ask the group if there is any factual proof that their solution is correct. This kind of slows everyone down for a minute as they consider the implications, as if wondering how to get around the inconvenience of having to support opinions with facts. But only for a moment.

Then, something pops into my mind unexpectedly. I don't know where it came from. Something I heard or read somewhere—radio, magazine, TV, newspaper. *A low frequency sound travels further.* The group has already overturned my request for supportive evidence and is busy lining up support for consensus. When the self-appointed leader turns to me, I see a look of apprehension in his eyes.

That's when I hit them with my unwelcome fact. It's like dropping a bomb. "It doesn't make sense…A low voice can't travel further than a high one….etc., etc.,…"

Where had I read it? they ask. Now that's a hard one—I can't remember. "What difference does it make?" I reply. Why can't they accept that I have some factual basis for making a decision and—seeing that no one else has any—shouldn't we base our choice on the only objective evidence we have? That's when the others start remembering that they *have* heard/read/recently-seen-a-report about high voices carrying further. I don't bother to ask where; we're deadlocked, 14 to 1, and time is running out. Somewhere—I can't remember where, but that isn't good enough for them. I become

100% committed and refuse to change my position, even when they argue for high and mighty consensus.

Before time runs out, I have converted a handful of fence-sitters. It's 10 to 5, and going my way. This enrages the 'high-pitched' majority. That, and not being able to come to a consensus. "I don't give a damn about consensus," I say. "The point of the exercise is to get it right."

"Reach a consensus," they holler.

It's small consolation to the majority when the session leaders inform us that a low-pitched voice is the correct answer. The ones for consensus are angry, and they stay angry with me for the remaining two days. I joke that at least we aren't dead—because, according to the facilitators, that's what would happen when their high-pitched screams couldn't reach the rescuers.

By now the facilitators are taking sardonic pleasure from the schism, believing that the greater the separation, the greater their triumph will be when the group is coaxed back to unity by the end of the three days. To quell the stir, they repeat the final instructions, to wit: *If you don't make the right choice, you'll be dead by morning.* The frustrated majority goes off to the break in a cloud of grumbles. The facilitators never do *recover* the group.

I'm left with a sense of foreboding. My little group of dissenters jumps up and down and slaps me on the back as if we'd just won an Olympic medal. I am disturbed. I picture myself in front of an imaginary group, talking about Kundalini to people with big, wide eyes. How would I manage their expectations? If this is any indication, people seem to prefer a joined-at-the-hip, feel-good experience to sallying forth on the lonely path. And that's why consensus is dangerous. Kundalini requires independent thinking, not dogmatic acceptance of the leader's will. That only ends in a disaster, like the Jonestown mob. On the other hand, who wants to hear about esoteric practices? Five people in the last century? In India?

• • •

I sell my interest in the school when I get accepted at a prestigious French business school. As soon as I graduate, one of my former customers offers me a job. I tell him I don't know anything about computer programming services. He insists I'm the person to open their branch office in the US. About the same time, a large French hotel chain offers me the job of Director of Worldwide Training. The former means setting up in the US; the latter means constant travel. For all my misgivings about integrating Kundalini into everyday life, things are looking up in the real world. I realize it's only an illusion, but that's the seductive power of even relative success.

Martine, on the other hand, is anxious, and doesn't really welcome either offer. In a pinch, she prefers the training job, because I won't have to move, just travel a lot. That way, she says, we can live in Paris and start the family she all of a sudden wants.

"I'm not so sure that fatherhood is a great idea. I don't feel entirely stable yet." What I stopped myself from saying was that I didn't want to become tied down in France for the duration of our children's educations. Even though Martine has renounced the French *bourgeoisie*, she might revert back once we have children. There are little giveaways, like the arguments and cajoling when I refuse to wear a coat and tie to dine at her parents' house.

"If we want to have children," she says, "we have to do it before I get past the age."

"Martine, I don't want children now."

Martine doesn't want to move to the US. She's not being difficult. She doesn't want to get locked down to an alien system. But with the offers bouncing around, I'm beginning to feel the tug of new perspectives. The training job is the safer bet, still I want to learn about computers. I know I'll never master computer programming, but I figure that my generalist background can help with the management side.

Martine and I are at an impasse: I want to take the offer and move to North Carolina. After a brief exploratory trip, Martine thinks it's a hopeless backwater and refuses to move. Funny how my attitude toward the south has changed since my Marine Corps days. But Charlotte is very different than Jacksonville, and the eighties are different than the fifties.

In the winter of 1982, leaving Martine in Paris, I take off for Charlotte, North Carolina. Stretched across two continents, we're more devoted to each other than ever. We talk regularly and write. I miss her. Fortunately, I have to return to Paris frequently for business purposes. This gives me the opportunity to prod Martine. But every time I think I've convinced her, she pulls back.

"I don't want to leave Paris," she says.

"Martine, with your experience, you could get your pick of jobs in the States. And when we move back to France, it would be a big item on your résumé. Besides, we'll be spending six weeks in Normandy every summer."

"You'd really want to move back to France?" she asks.

"Sure." It isn't a lie exactly, but I do enjoy living in the States. I've been away almost 15 years.

On the plane back to Charlotte, I realize that Martine will never agree to move. The rational approach won't work.

•   •   •

Three months go by. On my next trip to France, I arrange a layover in DC to visit my aunt. After she goes to bed, I decide to catch some live jazz at the One Step Down, a club I've been going to since my GW days.

Very crowded and noisy—so loud it makes my waitress lean in to hear my order. Our cheeks touch—just barely. A spark of human mortality jumps between us and later that night I am in her bed and she is making plans in the aftermath, going on a-mile-a-minute about our future. Not that I resist, I don't. It isn't just the allure of an unfamiliar body; my vigor has returned and after this long period of sexual inadequacy, suddenly I'm feeling supremely potent. Of course, I feel guilty about letting myself be waylaid. I can't blame Gloria. No, lying next to her, I'm not thinking about Kundalini, or anything else, only about the wonderful sex. In spite of my statements about being at peace with my sexuality, I don't want to do anything else except make love to her.

What a hypocrite! Now I'm trapped on two levels. Professionally, I want to insure the success of my mission, but deep down, I know that I am being called to something greater. Not to knock my job. The opportunity is turning my life around, but I have to find a way to educate people on Kundalini. Personally, of course, I've betrayed Martine.

When I return to France, there's the smell of another woman all over me. Maybe not the actual scent, but Martine grasps the situation and I don't dissemble. She tells me she knew it was coming. In spite of her objection to living in the US, abruptly she's ready to sacrifice to save our marriage.

"Okay, *chéri*, I'll come to North Carolina, if you agree to have children."

But I'm too absorbed in Gloria. "I have to let this thing play itself out," I say.

Which is really shorthand for hedging my bets. *If Gloria doesn't work out, I can always go back to Martine.* And even while I'm thinking this, I know I'm making a mistake. Pride, lust, vanity: somehow I'm able to rationalize the situation. But I'm only fooling myself, thinking I can keep two balls in the air.

"It's not going to end well," says Martine. "Relationships based on sex never do." Suddenly, she sounds like me. And I am stung, remembering all the times I justified my avoidance. I know Martine is right, yet I'm powerless to break the spell. The sex is just too good; it seems to validate me in a way I didn't think possible.

Yet in spite of the fact that I now ejaculate occasionally, the Kundalini never stops. It's always there to remind me of fundamentals. I don't have to philosophize, just listen to my body is all. Okay, I'm a lot stronger. Ejaculating doesn't have the same debilitating effect, but I'm still not to where Gopi Krishna predicted a *good sex life*. Shall I listen to my body, or do I start to disintegrate again?

Martine takes the practical approach. Once she rebounds from my betrayal, she issues me an ultimatum. On the last day of my visit, she tells me that if I go back to Gloria, it's over between us. She even tells me she's been seeing someone, adding she's willing to drop him, move to North Carolina, buy a house and start over. As she's speaking, I feel such love and respect for her. Here is a woman disciplined enough to put her own feelings aside in a bloody awful situation and motor on with the man who's betrayed her. Yet, even as she speaks, even as I feel such love and respect, I find myself being pulled under the orbit of sex—even with Gloria three thousand miles away. When I tell Martine I can't give up Gloria, I see the emotion well up in her face. One final tear and we're in bed for the last time. And it's the best ever between us, as if the lighting-in-a-bottle that I've captured with Gloria is now ubiquitously at my disposal.

Packing my bag the next morning, I think about the two women in my life and solemnly persuade myself that I'm doing the right thing. Martine doesn't really want to move to the States. And Gloria is really a great woman who'll do what I want, go where I go. But finally, it's Martine's prediction about the ultimate collapse of our relationship that makes me defiant and I find myself thinking I have to prove her wrong.

15—Integration

Now the news has arrived
From the Valley of Vail.
That a Chippendale Mupp has just bitten his tail,
Which he does every night before shutting his eyes.
Such nipping sounds silly. But, really, it's wise.
He has no alarm clock. So this is the way
He makes sure that he'll wake at the right time of day.
His tail is so long, he won't feel any pain
'Til the nip makes the trip and gets up to his brain.
In exactly eight hours, the Chippendale Mupp
Will, at last, feel the bite and yell "Ouch!" and wake up.

~ *Sleep Book*—Dr. Seuss

I'd like to say that our relationship flourishes, but it doesn't. It isn't Gloria's fault. She's a very spiritual person—lighthearted and effervescent. But Martine was right. A relationship based on sex can't last. I needed someone practical. Someone, well, someone like Martine, for instance—a partner who puts the couple's interests before anything else. Pity I didn't realize it.

Yet once Martine is out of my life, I realize how much I need to feel I am building something positive, a bone-deep connection. Gloria never communicates this. It's a very difficult, very subtle sensation to describe, knowing deep down the person you live with shares a common goal to the very core. And what matter the goal as long as it's shared. It's much more than the abstract notion of *being faithful*. I suppose I caught it during my time with Madeleine. When she left me, I developed a sixth sense, a kind of filter for testing each new relationship. Call it a defense mechanism. I can't quite put it into words, but when I'm with a woman who doesn't project it, I feel it, and immediately start to back off. I turn the filter off for Gloria. The sex is just too good.

My life is compartmentalized: the personal revolves around sex and the spiritual around my ongoing adjustment to Kundalini. There's nothing to hold us together. No sense of the practical. No hint of the attainable. Gloria is like a child hiding from the world. Slowly, I realize that, yes, we can copulate all night, but during the day we have nothing in common. No dreams, no feelings of mutual support. She wants to remain a child and I want to get away from the child who has haunted me. Yes, now that that child and I have made peace, I must get on with my life. Perhaps that's why Martine pushed me toward the ultimate responsibility of having children.

Gloria and I are short-lived. Over the next ten years I spend a lot of time by myself, integrating the various parts of my being. In my early fifties I meet Donna and we marry. As soon as we get settled, I start writing about the experience that changed my life.

• • •

The Kundalini has moved into the left side of my head and is pushing outward with tremendous force, and I realize I'm nearing the final stages of reconstruction. The fact that the two sides are close to balancing has two consequences. First, my body has nearly swelled to the limits of its template overlay. Second, my personality starts to change; I become more supple, more accommodating. The connection between personality and physical appearance is clear to me. I recall how in grammar school my personality subtly changed as my appearance changed. And I'm thinking how great it is to be nearing the end of the long road. Thirty years wandering in the desert and now the work is nearly finished. And as I'm thinking about it, at my moment of greatest triumph, my energy begins to falter.

No, not now, not at the end of my long ordeal.

It can't be. I'm almost there, and suddenly, it's as if I'm stuck. What's wrong? I think back to St. Jean. What saved me? My intuition. And I'm thinking if I ever needed intuition, I need it now.

It's not as if the Kundalini has stopped; it's working overtime, to no avail. Like I'm treading water, spinning my wheels. Must be all this expansion. And what fuels the expansion? Energy! That's it, I simply need more energy. I think back to St. Jean—to my final breakthrough. What was the decisive factor during the final awakening? After a moment it hits me. Why food, of course! Something must be wrong with my diet.

It's like having blinders suddenly torn from my eyes. For the past year I've been constipated, taking enzyme tablets for my digestion and Cascara Sagrada tablets and colonics to move my bowel. Funny, how difficult it is to see the things right before your eyes—how easy it is to stop listening to the body.

I can't stop with the tablets. Even though they're organic and natural, digestive aids are still not normal. I think about all the supplements I'm taking. Not just the ones for digestion, all the others, too. So many that I lose track of the names. What are they for? I thought I knew. Now I realize I'm all stopped up. Like someone put a cork in me—and the supplements don't seem to be making a difference.

I'm not a bad eater; in fact, I'm a slim 6'2" 190 pounds. I look around at all the overweight people and confidently tell myself I have no problem. I don't even feel bad. Sure there's the bowel and the digestive problems and a stuffed feeling on my left side, as if there's something stuck in my colon, but I'm not bad off. I'm just getting older.

I recall how sensitive to food the Kundalini was when I first activated it, and all of the adjustments I had to make to my diet. I remember thinking that sometime in the future, as the process neared completion, I'd be called on to make new adjustments. What adjustments? Become a vegetarian? Not likely. Been there, done that. I remember being tempted by forbidden dishes. Besides, meat may not be the most harmful element in my diet. Perhaps it's dairy or bread that's blocking me. There must be a perfect diet for Kundalini. So, what is it?

Nothing comes to me, not a glimmer, not a hint. No intuitive insights. I let things slide, continuing to rely on supplements. And all the time I'm thinking: what I'm eating must be really bad for the colon. Bagels and cream cheese for breakfast, a lot of bread and cereal. Dairy products. Gosh, this can't be good, stuffing the colon with a lot of mucus. And even though I've stopped eating a lot of meat, perhaps I don't eat enough fruit and vegetables. But I eat fruit and vegetables. Nevertheless, something's stuffing me up. So how can I change it?

Well, by falling back on the invincibility of the Kundalini is how. At least, that's what I tell myself. Hey, I have this restorative power living inside me. It's invincible. It will take care of me. Kundalini can overcome anything. Well, no, it can't overcome sabotage to your own body. So the whole thing has me feeling depressed. And hey, that's not me; I never get depressed. If I'd been prone to depression, I'd never have made it through St. Jean. In my anxiety I turn to frequent colonics. Sure they clean me out temporarily, but they don't have a lasting effect. Is this the way I'm supposed to live the rest of my life? Eat, take supplements, get pumped out, only to eat some more?

• • •

I pull into the parking lot of the Co-op near my home and I'm about to kill the engine. Something on the radio stops me. A young Russian woman is talking about digestive enzymes on the local NPR station. What she says catches my attention. I turn off the motor, sit back to listen.

She's advocating a diet based on raw foods. Her name is Victoria Boutenko. Something about how cooking kills the natural digestive enzymes in foods. All at once, I get that great feeling of intuitive certainty, knowing when something is right without analyzing it. It doesn't happen often, but when it does, it leaps out at me.

After enzymes, she talks about her family's health problems. It's like a catalogue of modern American degenerative diseases: diabetes, asthma, rheumatoid arthritis, indigestion, obesity, lack of energy, mood swings, hyperthyroid, dental problems and arrhythmia. And though she doesn't mention it, I know the raw foods concept extends to colon care, and probably many other afflictions.

Perhaps it's her empirical approach, the same approach that led me to Kundalini. Intuitively knowing something's right, and having enough faith to try it. When she speaks about rejecting insulin injections for her son's diabetes, it resonates. After many failed cures, months of research, she comes across an idea that resonates. She tries it on herself and her family. It works for them just like Kundalini worked for me.

At least I don't spend money on the supplements I was intending to buy. I leave the health food store with two bags of fresh fruit. When I get home, I go on the Internet and order two of Victoria's books. Unfortunately, only a few days before, I spent $400 on Trader Joe's specialty foods. But I decide to go cold turkey. Donna and the rest of my family can have a field day with the gourmet delicacies.

A few days later, Victoria Boutenko's book, *12 Steps to Raw Foods*, arrives. Two hours later, I prepare my first raw meal. I'll have to get some new equipment, but my raw soup is pretty good.

I feel a little weak for the first couple of days after the changeover, yet don't notice any lack of energy during Yoga or meditation. By the end of the week, I'm having regular bowel movements and no digestive problems. What's more, unlike my vegetarian experience, I'm not tempted by the restaurant signs or the cooked dishes my family prepares. I go about my business in one corner of the kitchen while they go about theirs. Of course, my son makes comments. That's to be expected. Is there anyone in our society more addicted to cooked food than a 13-year-old? Over time, I'll try to sensitize him the benefits of raw foods, right now he's not open to persuasion.

The ideal platform for Kundalini is the fittest possible dwelling. A pure host body. The least corrupted, the least run down. If I can't influence the timetable of the Kundalini, at least I can influence the environment it works in. And something tells me that over the next few months, my new diet is going to supercharge the Kundalini.

In one week, I'm a 100% raw fooder. Hey, I don't like to drag things out. Perhaps it's all the bad habits I've had to overcome.

12 Steps to Raw Foods opens my eyes to cooked food as an addiction. Cigarettes, alcohol, drugs, sex, bad food! I'm hoping that I'm finally rid of them, but I don't underestimate their power. The current addiction is always harder to break than the previous one. Are cooked foods the last of my addictions? A month ago I would have laughed if someone had told me eating cooked food was an addiction. But it all starts with the gut. If the gut is blocked, it becomes loaded with impurities and, most likely, you're not eliminating after every meal. To people conditioned to supplements and laxatives, elimination after every meal sounds impossible. Believe me, it isn't. Regular elimination should be the norm. Read *The Cure is the Cause* by Dr. Ruza Bogdanovich, ND. Among the many authors on degenerative diseases, Dr. Ruza stands out in her ability to explain the fundamental importance of a clean gut.

What exactly is a degenerative disease? Just more confusing medical terminology? I like Dr. Ruza's definition: degenerative disease occurs when the body does not get what it needs. When it doesn't, it degenerates. Take diabetes, she says. We don't inherit diabetes; we inherit the habits that cause diabetes. Namely, a harmful cooked foods diet.

No wonder I never thought of cooked food as harmful! Cooking is one of life's most respected traditions. Why, the very thought of cooked food is comforting! So much so that in order to help people overcome its addictive power, Victoria has organized her book like the AA Bible—The Twelve Steps.

I used to think that the time when one hits 'rock bottom' depends on the depth of despair and closeness to death. Do you also think so? Then I have good news for you; nothing is further from the truth! Have you noticed that everyone hits 'rock bottom' at different levels of addiction? Some people get emphysema before they quit smoking, some are able to quit at a very early age of addiction, and some lose everything and die but never quit. That means hitting 'rock bottom' is not connected to disease and despair but to something else. What? What is the magic wand that returns people back to the fullness of life? It is called THE POWER OF ADMITTING. In other words, facing the truth.[38]

• • •

Six months after I started the raw foods diet, the final chapter of my adventure began. And once it started, it took only a short while to complete. Not only did the raw foods diet cleanse my gut, it kicked my Kundalini into high gear. Now, like a rocket aimed at a far-away star, I've intersected with the original design of my perfect body. The stretching and pulling and reshaping are finished. In one final burst of titanic energy, I've become whole. At long last I'm living the promise of perfection imagined before my birth.

I don't want to go too far, too fast. The wonder of it is too new. I want to stay away from exaggerated claims. Raw fruit and vegetables not only make me feel better, they work with the Kundalini. Am I certain that I will continue my 100% raw foods diet? I don't know. At times, the Kundalini seems to be ordering me to eat particular foods. I'm not talking about doughnuts and Monster Thickburgers, but pickled beets, warm vegetable soups or yogurt.

It's great to sit in meditation once again and have the light come on steady and strong, with no stretching and tearing at the sinews. Still, I marvel at the finesse of Kundalini. It could have torn me apart thirty years ago, but the whole process was so perfectly regulated, not one nerve or muscle or bone was damaged.

That's because there's a logic to Kundalini. Why else has this amazing mechanism been included in the body's arsenal of healing tools? A design flaw or an evolutionary mistake? Hardly. Whether it's always been part of the body or it evolved slowly, it's there, just like the prehensile thumb. And just like the prehensile thumb, it's a practical tool for personal evolution, first and foremost for healing our abused and mistreated bodies. That's right, before we wish for anything fancy, like expanding consciousness, visions of dancing monkeys, or merging with the Creator, we can heal ourselves. Kundalini provides a second chance, like a warranty, a mechanism for healing our world-weary bodies.

As the end came closer, I knew there would be a *pop*. Sure enough, during the final days, as the energy surged through every part of my body, circulating through my entire nervous system, it exerted tremendous pressure against the inner surface of my head. Like dents in a metal tank or casing forced outward under extreme air pressure, the unbalanced regions of my head popped into perfect symmetrical balance. Right on cue, the rest of my body followed, filling into its predetermined shape.

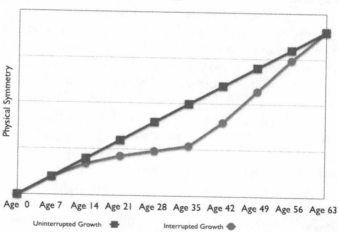

As I watched the inner light heal my defects and restore my symmetry, I realized it was as far as *The Secret of the Golden Flower* could take me. Its secret wisdom has returned me to the being I was destined to become.

Epilogue

To me individually, to my heart has been revealed a knowledge beyond all doubt, unattainable by reason, and here I am obstinately trying to express that knowledge in reason and words.

~ Anna Karenina—Leo Tolstoy

I could have recreated myself as a healer who dispenses cures, or as a mystic who deals in spiritual doubletalk. But that isn't who I have become; it isn't me. It took me a long time to write this book, first, because I'm still working with Kundalini, and second, because I'm still struggling to understand it.

Most of all, I'm wary of those who claim special powers or ecstatic visions. I want to confine myself to the healing properties of Kundalini because they can be observed in a scientific manner. And while fantastic powers and expanded consciousness are surely due to Kundalini, physical integrity is more than I could have ever imagined.

The Healing Power of Kundalini

You don't have to wait for an auto accident to become crippled. Your own mind is capable of deforming you—if you let it. My deformity was self-induced, caused by my willful refusal to reveal the presence of a splinter, effectively shutting off vital growth energy to parts of my body. How prevalent are nervous disorders? "Nerves can be damaged by alcohol, drugs, too much glucose in the blood (as in one form of diabetes), too much vitamin B6, arsenic, mercury, lead, and organophosphate residues (from weed killers). They can also be damaged by vitamin deficiencies, especially of the B vitamins; or damage may be a consequence of infections such as shingles, diphtheria, polio, tetanus, or leprosy or of vaccines, as in Guillain-Barré syndrome. Some form of neuropathy affects one person in 400; symptoms range from mild tingling to agonizing or shooting pains, and from pins and needles to complete numbness and wasting of unused muscles. Weakness and loss of sensation can easily result in injury."[39]

Can Kundalini treat nerve related conditions like polio aftereffects, surgical displacements, arthritis, chronic pain, migraine headaches, muscular and ligament problems, neural irregularities, neuritis or neuralgia? I know it revitalized my nervous system and flooded vital growth energy through my entire being in order to straighten my deformed body.

Now any doctor reading this is going to start foaming at the mouth and ask, "How can this guy be so irresponsible?" And I understand his skepticism. But we're dealing with empirical science, a system the medical profession, by and large, refuses to accept. Yet it's older than modern medicine, older even than material science. Material science has produced a one-step forward, two-steps back movement throughout history. With the Salk vaccine, we get the atom bomb. And most of the time we only find out much later that the vaccines or artificial fertilizers we thought were so great have harmful side effects. More important, material science is out of my control. Its controllers won't let me look behind the curtain and see who's running the show. And who is? Yogi Berra? The Wizard of Oz? Whoever it is, I have to accept their declarations on faith, and that's not acceptable. I want to be in charge of my body.

The kicker is, empirical science works. Ask the people who have tried it. There are thousands of success stories. So when I hear the medical community condemning "unproven" results and methods that do not stand up to scientific inquiry, I ask, "What about the medical community? How well does it stand up to scrutiny?"

I have no quarrel with doctors or the medical profession. Most medical procedures are beneficial; most doctors are competent. I couldn't set a broken leg. Nor could I help a victim of a car crash. I'm not qualified to judge medical procedures or research. But even in the mainstream there is near unanimity that the medical experience is less than satisfactory. In fact, a recent study suggests that it's downright unsafe, statistically speaking, that is:

> A definitive review and close reading of medical peer-review journals, and government health statistics shows that American medicine frequently causes more harm than good. The number of people having in-hospital, adverse drug reactions (ADR) to prescribed medicine is 2.2 million. Dr. Richard Besser, of the CDC, in 1995, said the number of unnecessary antibiotics prescribed annually for viral infections was 20 million. Dr. Besser, in 2003, now refers to tens of millions of unnecessary antibiotics. The number of unnecessary medical and surgical procedures performed annually is 7.5 million.

The number of people exposed to unnecessary hospitaliza-
tion annually is 8.9 million. The total number of iatrogenic[40]
deaths is 783,936. It is evident that the American medical
system is the leading cause of death and injury in the United
States. The 2001 heart disease annual death rate is 699,697;
the annual cancer death rate, 553,251.[41]

I often overhear remarks such as, "I never take my kids to the
doctor" or "I just tough it out." Most likely, you've heard mothers
express similar reservations—right up to the moment when little
Davey sneezes. But as soon as the crying and the pain kick in, it's
off to the doctor. I understand this. What other options do people
have? Yet each time a mother succumbs, she feels uncomfortable, as
if somehow she should have resisted. I know I do. The experience
just isn't very pleasant. The arrogance of many doctors, the refusal
to listen to patients, the 'expert know-it-all' attitude. Not to mention the many instances of misdiagnosis and incompetence.

Does this mean that I will never again visit the doctor—even
though, at this moment, I feel secure in the cleansing power of raw
foods and Kundalini? To be honest, I can't say I'll never again visit the
doctor, but one thing's for sure, I want to lessen the chances of future
medical visits. What about you? Now that you've seen how loss of
music and math ability led me to discover my structural deformity,
think how easy it is to detect a dysfunctional gut. All it takes, in most
cases, is admitting that you feel bad after a heavy cooked meal, especially if you have to *wash* it down with a load of laxatives.

Now I realize how difficult it is to admit the truth, especially
at a time when fast foods are staging a counterattack à la *Meat on
meat on meat*! Ruby Tuesday's has dropped nearly one-third of their
40 original healthy eating options. And nutritional information
now appears only for the remaining healthy items, which have been
relegated to the back of the menu. Richard Johnson, senior vice-
president, notes that the restaurant's chicken tenders, fries, ribs and
burgers still top the bestseller lists.

"That's the way Americans eat," he says, "even if they claim to
want healthier options."[42] In effect, the fast-food chains are daring
the American people to be consistent—and betting that they won't
be. "Hardee's target consumer doesn't care about calories. One of

the restaurant's most popular items: two-thirds of a pound of pure Angus beef, plus bacon, cheese, and mayonnaise served on a buttered bun. The 1,410-calorie Monster Thickburger, which was launched at the end of last year, is hailed by Steve Lemley, vice-president of marketing, as 'a monument to decadence, something to eat that isn't necessarily politically correct.' Decadence indeed. At fast-food and family restaurants across the country, big-calorie, high-fat food is back with a vengeance."[43]

The fast food industry is betting it can keep us addicted to harmful cooked foods. And why not? We've never shown we could resist. Perhaps that's why food producers are now marketing foods especially for those people who are leery of drugs and additives. According to a recent *New York Times* article, "Marketing surveys show that more Americans are interested in natural solutions to health problems."

"People are getting nervous about pharmaceuticals," said Faith Popcorn, who runs BrainReserve, a marketing company. "If it's food, people trust it more. And people are always so happy to hear that something they love to eat is also good for them." People want natural cures. The problem is there aren't many real cures, and the ones that work aren't readily available.

I've had a chance to put my experience in perspective, to see empirical science and Kundalini as practical tools for healing stress, aging effects, illness and general mistreatment of the body. Yet so much of Kundalini literature talks about oneness and expanding consciousness. These are highly subjective concepts; they are difficult to understand and verify. Does that mean they're not worth pursuing? No, it doesn't. But they're religious concepts; Kundalini is empirical science where cleansing and healing of the physical body come first.

Before you consider Kundalini, ask yourself: What are you looking for? Magic? Genius? Special powers? Enlightenment? Higher consciousness? If you are, perhaps you're getting ahead of yourself. While there's no doubt Kundalini plays a role in the evolution of consciousness, any incremental jump in consciousness, be it collective or individual, may be some way off. My program focuses on the one thing Kundalini can accomplish right now, namely healing the body and resisting addiction.

Golden Flower Meditation: Safe Kundalini Activation

Yes, there are some horror stories surrounding Kundalini. There are also horror stories about pharmaceuticals, face creams, daycare centers and automobiles. So is Golden Flower Meditation (GFM) safe? Is driving a car safe? Is airplane travel safe? Are prescription medicines safe? I can only say that GFM worked for me, and over time, I learned to live with Kundalini and to marvel at its miraculous healing powers.

Will GFM work for you? GFM isn't for everyone. A good test for deciding whether GFM is for you is by weighing the stakes. How much do you want to cleanse and purify your body, to repair neural disorders and the systems those nerves serve? Do you have other options? What is the overall cost of trying each option? In my case, GFM was the only option.

Just remember one thing: Kundalini was incorporated into our beings for a reason; otherwise it wouldn't be there. So why all the horror stories? Well, I've studied the so-called horror stories, and quite simply most of them stem from the haphazard approaches used in awakening Kundalini. And that's exactly why we should be wary of horror stories. Not only are the results varied, they are often incomplete. Moreover, many awakenings have only been temporary. That's not to say that they weren't useful, interesting or genuine. They were. However, to produce a completely permanent awakening, the method for raising Kundalini must be standardized.

Can GFM produce standardized results? GFM is based on the 'backward-flowing method,' an ancient breath control procedure that entails reversing the direction of the breath at a certain point in time during the meditation process—about 100 days in. The *autopilot* aspect of the 'backward-flowing method' brings a needed element of standardization to the process and assures a permanent outcome.

What do I mean by autopilot? The Ram Dass saying, "First *you do it*, then *it does you*," is an apt description of how the process works. When you start GFM, you focus on diaphragmatic deep breathing. Then, at a certain point in time—one I clearly describe how to recognize—you reverse the direction of your breath. From that point forward, you're on autopilot; you no longer have to focus on breathing or anything else. An inner mechanism—part of the Kundalini-Life Force process—takes over. Instead of *you doing it, it does you*. It's like the unseen ground controller that guides your flight to a safe landing.

Once I activated my Kundalini, my life went back to normal: eating, digestion, drinking, stress levels, exercise and sleep. Kundalini had become a permanent part of my somatic functions.

I had my ups and downs, but awakening Kundalini is a trade-off, in my case, a choice I was willing to make. I traded my potential to copulate at will for the capability of channeling sexual energy into my brain, a trade-off that allowed me to revitalize my entire nervous system, and subsequently rebuild my body according to its perfect blueprint.

The Golden Flower Meditation (GFM) Method

The goal of GFM is to standardize the outcome of the Kundalini-Life Force activation process. In other words, to make one Kundalini experience indistinguishable from another. And although this may not be 100% possible at the moment, I believe that GFM comes close to meeting this objective. Why? Because it's based on the backward-flowing method, a technique perfected by the ancients over a long period of time, several centuries, in fact. Validation is simply a fact of more individuals practicing GFM.

GFM demands commitment, self-discipline and concentration of the kind you'd expect from a doctorate level program. To undertake it, you must be sufficiently advanced in living empirical sciences. Proficiency with diaphragmatic deep breathing is required. In fact, it's a prerequisite for any serious meditation method. It takes training to develop diaphragmatic deep breathing. I don't have space for it in this book, but in the future I will post relevant information on my website <www.lifeforcebooks.com>.

Most important, you must be ready for GFM. How do you know if you're ready? That's the tricky part. Your state of readiness is not something I, or any other person, can determine. Only your body can tell you. And it will, if you know how to listen to it.

1. Check your symmetry.

Q: What's so important about symmetry?

A: "Symmetry means being the same, or even, on each side. Over the last few years, biologists have looked at the animal kingdom, and they've made a few discoveries about symmetry, and how it relates to beauty and fitness.

"First, animals that are more symmetrical are more likely to attract a mate. One scientist found that he could turn attractive male swallows into unattractive male swallows (and also ruin their chances of a good sex life) by clipping their tail feathers with scissors.

"Secondly, symmetry influences fitness. Horses that are more symmetrical run faster than horses that are less symmetrical. In one study, biologists measured some ten features on 73 thoroughbreds—features such as the thickness of the knee, or the width of the nostrils. The differences they could measure were quite small, and probably had nothing directly to do with how fast the horse could run. In fact, symmetry is probably a good indicator of general health and strength. Our imperfect world is full of nasty chemicals and germs. Only those individuals that are lucky enough to inherit a sturdy genetic makeup, and are also lucky enough to get good nutrition while they're growing, will end up being more symmetrical."[44]

Get the point? Symmetry more or less guarantees unblocked nerve channels and balanced growth.

Q: I'm not symmetrical, what can I do about it?

A: If you're not symmetrical, something must have happened. After my accident, my symmetrical body became asymmetrical. I gambled, and Kundalini restored my symmetry. It's up to you to understand the commitment and evaluate the effort.

Q: How do I check my symmetry?

A: There are various means of checking symmetry:

1. Musical ability, rhythm. The ability to sing notes with proper intonation.

2. Mathematical ability, computer programming.

3. Sports. Especially balancing sports such as skateboarding, target sports, ice-skating, gymnastics, bicycling, tightrope walking, juggling.

4. Kirlian photography.[45]

5. Regular photography, a process you can undertake yourself. Here's how:

Take a portrait-sized photo of yourself. Scan the negative into your computer, load it into Photoshop, and crop the image until the face is tightly enclosed in the frame. Drop a line down the exact center of your face, cut the image in two, then separate the two sides. Duplicate each side, and drag the two left and two right sides together. Flip the duplicate horizontally and nudge until it's vertically aligned with its corresponding other half. What you have, in each case, are faces composed of two instances of the left side and two instances of the right side, one half merely flipped to complete the image. Here are sample images taken by a couple of Australian teachers. Study each composite image and compare it with the original.

"After much thought an Art teacher at school and I worked out a way to find out. We photographed some of the children and then through a bit of 'darkroom magic' manipulated them. You'll notice that the photos of each child's face is made up of the original photo, 2 left sides and 2 right sides."[46]

Right/Right   Left/Left   Original Photo

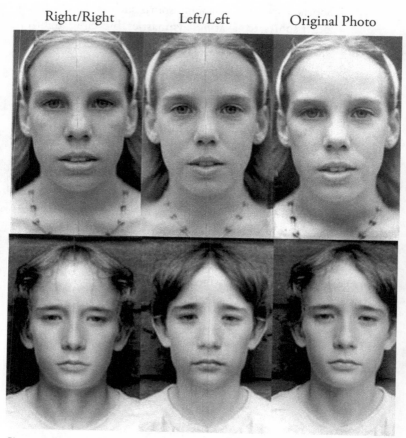

Figure 4: **Some Faces are More Symmetrical than Others**

Note. Failure to pass any of the above tests does not constitute a lack of symmetry or mean that you are not apt to undertake Kundalini training. There are other determinants, namely your own resolve and fortitude.

2. Get clean!

This means a raw foods diet! You can't heal on a poor foundation. This was the one issue hindering both Gopi Krishna and myself. So learn from our mistakes. By the way, even if you decide not to undertake Kundalini, this step should be a keeper.

Why? Let's take a closer look at the relationship between a raw foods diet and Kundalini. What do these two healing therapies have in common? Well, nothing secret or cryptic. In fact, a little common sense reveals that both rely on ingested substances. For a raw foods diet, it's the food and drink we consume; for Kundalini, it's the air we breathe. One, food and drink converted to sugar; two, properties in the air that our bodies convert to Prana.

I won't go into the science of nutrition or Prana[47]. There are researched volumes full of relevant materials. Let's just say that both therapies use and process the elements we introduce into our bodies. So it's up to us to make sure these elements are pure.

3. Meditate.

I can't personally supervise your practice, but here are the steps culled from my own experience with *The Secret of the Golden Flower*.

1. Sit in Lotus position.

2. Drop a plumb-line, that is, find your center as described on pages 34–35 in *The Secret of the Golden Flower*—the bit about the tip of your nose.

3. Block out the 10,000 things by counting your breath in a regular 4/4 cadence. Inhale 4 counts, hold 4, exhale 4, hold 4 counts. Start over. Instead of trying to form a *Lotus Petal* in perfect detail or contemplate *Compassion*, I advise counting. Why? Because it occupies your mind just enough to forestall the 10,000 things. At the same time, it doesn't require you to do something out of reach—like mystical contemplation. Little by little, the counting will fall away of its own accord and your mind will be still.

4. Do this regularly each morning, preferably before eating.

5. When you notice air current movement in the lower belly as you inhale (about 100 days in), reverse your breath (the backward-flowing method).

6. In a few days, you'll be on autopilot. That is, you won't be able to change the direction of your breath back again. Nature (the Primal Spirit) will reassume control.

For reference, buy a copy of *The Secret of the Golden Flower* and *Kundalini: The Evolutionary Energy in Man*.

4. Remember to keep a strict raw foods diet.

This is the most frequent source of problems in the later stages, so be sure to stay raw. Raw foods produce the vital, easily digestible energy you need to fuel your Kundalini. Even small amounts of raw fruits and vegetables provide a lot of energy, including hormones, oxygen, enzymes, vitamins and minerals. Cooked food provides only the last two elements.

5. Wait for further orders.

You have returned the Life Force (the Primal Spirit) to its place of rightful sovereignty. The Self (the Conscious Spirit) is no longer in charge. The Primal Spirit created you; it won't let you get in trouble if you listen to it. Not that the Conscious Spirit won't try to "seduce" you into doing things the "old familiar way." It will. Just sit back and wait for further orders. They will come! Not out of "the burning bush," but from your body. It's the body you should be listening to.

Paying Dues

My approach to Kundalini has always been: keep it real, down-to-earth, and, above all, human. Don't feel you have to become *more spiritual* before attempting it. That's putting the cart before the horse. You can't change your personality just like that—suddenly becoming more wholesome, more spiritual. Once you activate it, Kundalini will take care of spiritual attitudes. In fact, there should be no conflict between your religion and the empirical science you use to awaken your Kundalini.

Trying to change your personality is like trying to drive a car before your foot can reach the pedals. So don't try, no matter how many articles you read in so-called spiritual periodicals. Articles with titles like: *The Path of Peace, Kindness and Compassion* and *Searching the Heart for Tranquility* are meant to make you feel unworthy, that you can't possibly live up to the lofty ideals of feeling compassionate or experiencing universal love. And you are right; nobody can, or very few people can. Because right now, where you are in your pursuit of living empirical knowledge, you may not be able to achieve these things, not on any meaningful, permanent basis, not without paying your dues. That's where living empirical science comes in. It teaches you to rely on your experience, to understand what you've accomplished.

What's more, you don't know anything about the people who write these articles. Who are they? How evolved are they—from a living empirical science perspective, that is? You'd have to spend time with them to find out. Many of them are just running a lot of spiritual smack. Ask yourself: What are they after? Are they citing opinions or facts? I've met lots of people who talk a good game, but then can't deliver the goods.

My approach, on the other hand, isn't based on who you are, what you've done or what you think. It's about doing and results. Notice that these articles never give you any practical information about how to reach the lofty goals the authors talk about. That's because the great melting pot of spiritual seekers is as lost as the great melting pot of NASCAR fans. That's why we have aberrations like Jonestown—because individuals are looking for someone to take responsibility over their lives. Someone with charisma! My program demands that **you** take responsibility for acquiring your own empirical self-knowledge.

When you activate the Life Force, you'll begin to see changes, not only in your physical body, but also in your entire being—your emotions, your outlook, as well as your psychological and spiritual attitudes. So don't give away your Power. Live the life you were meant to live, without holding back.

Science vs. Science

The baseless arguments between the opposing factions supporting Intelligent Design and evolution amuse me. Who says that an entity that designs life is not willing or capable of letting it evolve? From 1972 to 1985, the Renault 5 (*Le Car* in the USA) was one of the world's most successful cars. In fact, its sales remained strong because the design of the car evolved to fit the needs of its consumers. Design and evolution, as most industrialists know, are not mutually exclusive. Why should living beings be any different? So what if our species has evolved from mud? There was a plan for the mud, just like there's a plan for individual substantiation, just like there's a plan for me and for you. Do I believe in Intelligent Design? I believe there is an entity at work creating designs in nature. Why? Because I've seen it at work! Do I accept the material scientific research on evolution? Of course! Why? Because as an aware, sentient person, I'm able to understand both empirical and rational proofs.

There's no reason that the two cannot coexist. Moreover, the whole debate is a waste of time. The real question is: Do we do everything in our conscious power to assure that the plan for our unique bodily substantiation reaches fruition? And if not, do we have a plan to repair, regenerate and heal our bodies? A plan to extend our consciousness?

The debate really boils down to an argument between the mind and the body, between the talkers and the doers. Each side has its proponents. The ones who say the craziest things—like preventing mudslides with crystals—get the most attention. The disagreement, however, stems from indignation. Side A is offended by Side B's approach to science, and vice-versa. Why? Because, once again, we've been conditioned through family, education, church and culture to believe that *our* approach is correct; i.e., if our approach is right, the other side must be wrong.

It's time the two sides were on speaking terms. One can't exist without the other. I couldn't have made it through my Kundalini experience without my mind. There are always things to figure out, and that's the job of the mind: to concentrate, to analyze, to associate, to extrapolate, to think laterally and logically.

I would never have been able to discover the rightful significance of the *backward-flowing method* without the associative and deductive powers of the mind.

Does My Experience Relate to You?

I've stopped doing the foolish, self-destructive things I used to do. I could have kept them to myself, made no open confession. So, why did I? Well, I decided that for my story to become relevant, it needed "real-world" exposure. I want you to see how easy it is to sink below the surface and how important it is to not give up. But why mix the sacred with the shameful? Because the shameful moments are often the turning points of our lives.

Yes, the power of admitting seems to kick in when we most need it. Not always, but sometimes. So just because we lose our way, doesn't mean we can't find it again. In fact, I see my life as a series of arcs, one a shadow life, parallel to my other real flesh and blood life. As I look back on my *real life*, it seems less substantial—as if someone else had done those things. And that's the magic of rebirth.

Like a cancer patient who's been given a book on raw foods, I was given a book—*The Secret of the Golden Flower*, the perfect formula for correcting my basal structural defects. Nothing else could have corrected my condition—not Yoga, diet, prayer, Sufism, surgery or psychoanalysis—only living empirical science, which is based on the principles of *non-action through action*, the strongest scientific principle in the universe.

Who wants to live a life like mine? Sometimes accidents, like chemical spills, are the means to new discoveries. So if my discoveries are meaningful, I'll accept my life as an accident in a Petrie dish. The only thing I left behind was a shallow world of privilege.

As it was, I might have been just another conformist, a guy with all the advantages. A lawyer or investment banker. Someone who declines to do anything special. Instead, on account of my deformity, I blazed new karmic trails, like Orpheus descending into the vortex of his greatest fears. What other choice did I have? Where else would I have found living empirical scientific knowledge? In the salons of mainline suburban Philadelphia or in Bedford, New

York—places where everything's fine as long as the stock market, real estate prices, and pork bellies are going up? Not likely!

In fact, I believe my recovery boiled down to never letting anyone or anything deter me from finding my way back to my true self. In short, I never gave up on Perfection.

> The greatest book in the world, the Mahabharata, tells us we all have to live and die by our karmic cycle. Thus works the perfect reward-and-punishment, cause-and-effect, code of the universe. We live out in our present life what we wrote out in our last. But the great moral thriller also orders us to rage against karma and its despotic dictates. It teaches us to subvert it. To change it. It tells us we also write out our next lives as we live out our present.[48]

The Future of Kundalini

In his later books and speeches, Gopi Krishna encouraged the scientific investigation of Kundalini and a dialogue with the scientific community.[49] How useful is scientific research into Kundalini? If it allows a dialogue between the two schools of science, it might be very useful.

Nevertheless, I believe the time for a synthesis between material and empirical science has not yet arrived. One day soon it may. In the meantime, we don't need the approbation of the scientific community. I believe that empirical science must build up its credentials by making the Kundalini experience reliable and safe. Empirical science has lagged behind material science because it got labeled as a pseudo-religion—spiritualism, or some indistinct offshoot.

Religion concerns matters of faith. Scientists, whether material or empirical scientists, should be free to believe what they want. But their beliefs should not affect their scientific investigation. I prefer to be known as a scientist, a man who studies healing and consciousness, albeit from a different perspective.

Certainly, no one has done more to advance the understanding of Kundalini than Gopi Krishna. His masterwork, *Kundalini: The Evolutionary Energy in Man,* is still, after almost forty years, the only book of its kind. His many years of living with Kundalini, his clairvoyance, his big picture outlook, his ability to frame the debate on Kundalini, set him apart. Nevertheless, as he tried to elevate the debate to the level of scientific inquiry, he became trapped in polemics over the validity of the Kundalini experience and the authenticity of Prana, as if the material scientists who demanded verification of his accounts were on equal footing.

Remember these scientists come from the same tradition as the ones who recently decided that chills cause colds. For years scientists had been telling us that links between chilling and viral infection have "no scientific basis." Now, according to a recent UK study, they've changed their minds. Wow, I figured that one out for myself at the age of six. Does their turn-around mean all scientific research is flawed or incomplete? No, it simply means that we can figure some things out by ourselves. Just as Gopi Krishna did. Here's a man pioneering investigation into one of the most complex unexplained systems in the universe and material scientists tell him Kundalini is all in the mind and Prana's not verifiable.

I'm not against scientists. They apply a method to prove a hypothesis. A good method, a time-tested method, a method involving hypothesis, proof and evidence. Problems only arise with the method when scientists find no evidence to support a given hypothesis. Then they conclude that the hypothesis is invalid. Sometimes this leads to ridicule. A link between colds and chilling? Ridiculous! How could anybody be so dumb? There's no connection between the common cold and chilling—unless we tell you there is. No connection between Kundalini and neural regeneration either. No such element as Prana in the air we breathe.

The problem is the evidence is not always right out in the open. It may be evidence one cannot measure statistically or see under a microscope. Sometimes it's buried deep inside the body, where only "knowers" of the body can perceive it. Does that mean it does not exist? According to material scientists, YES.

But the link between the common cold and chilling has always been there, even before material scientists officially recognized it. So, you see, the material scientific view of the world is largely built on supposition and premise, not on reality. When it comes to knowing Kundalini, these scientists aren't on equal footing with Gopi Krishna. Sure, they are experts in their fields, but they have never had a Kundalini experience, or even a little jolt that changed their perspective and made them more aware. Many scientists have, you know. Men like Albert Hoffmann, the discoverer of LSD. A man who, according to the *New York Times*, once said, "Any natural scientist who was not a mystic was not a real natural scientist."

So you have material scientists telling Gopi Krishna, an individual who lived with Kundalini for forty years, that his experience was only an extension of his imagination, driving him to the point where, in his later writings, we find him exclaiming: "Now a material scientist may argue that, well, we have gained this consciousness by experience. Why has not the ox or the cow or the fish gained it?

"Then he will argue that, well, man's consciousness took a leap, but when we ask him how did it take a leap, he is dumb. He knows nothing. Even Darwin had to admit that we could give no definite explanation for it except that it is part of natural selection. So you see the whole structure of materialistic philosophy has been built on suppositions and premises, not on realities.

"The first reality we come across is consciousness. The world comes later. We know first ourselves and then the world. So the wiser course is first to understand the knower. What modern thinkers have done is to ignore or bypass the knower, forgetting that it is the knower that is doing it."[50] This is a very scientific statement. There's a lot to be done in getting "to know" the knower.

The real problem for empirical science has been a lack of a single coherent method for its practitioners to rally around. Gopi Krishna suggested that Kundalini was the biological basis of religion. I submit that Kundalini is not only the biological basis of religion, but of empirical science, the antecedent of both religion and material science.

I realized this after reading *The Secret of the Golden Flower*. Not at first, however. No, because of its arcane language and Taoist overtones, at first, I thought it was a "spiritual" document. Nevertheless, as I began practicing its method of meditation, I recognized that this book dealt more with the laws of science than the canons of religion. It described a method capable of reproducing the same results over and over, no matter the religious beliefs or cultural predispositions of the practitioner. You see, *The Secret of the Golden Flower* is really a science book. I call it *The Empirical Science Bible*, using the word bible not in a religious sense, but in a comprehensive informational sense, like a programmer's *The Standard C++ Bible*.

I got to thinking, if the empirical approach is to be considered a science, it must employ the paraphernalia of a science. And it does. While material science uses microscopes and computers, centrifuges and cyclotrons, chemical formulae, test tubes and beakers to perform experiments on material objects, empirical science uses meditation, Yoga, Kundalini, self-observation, and the trained, observant mind to perform experiments with the knower.

So if GFM can be perfected as a reliable method, on a par with the scientific method, a synthesis between modern material and living empirical science can be achieved.

Currently, the Institute for Consciousness Research, whose work is based on Gopi Krishna's legacy, proposes the following:

1. Analysis of case studies of persons suffering from mental disturbances.

2. Interviews with physicians, psychiatrists, and social workers involved with care of the mentally disturbed.

3. Worldwide advertising outlining the classic symptoms of Kundalini, calling on experienced people to come forward.

4. A clinic to treat and support individuals undergoing a Kundalini-type process.[51]

For me, Points 1 or 2 entail too much non-empirical research, information that must be put through the filter of third-party interpretation. So also Point 3 whose diverse experiences would be a nightmare to interpret and classify. It's Point 4 that really interests me because I am eager to see GFM perform in a scientifically controlled test setting.

GFM enables an individual to raise Kundalini in a few months. Is it the only valid approach? No, but it's the only one I know. I can vouch for it. As for avoiding pitfalls, I've studied them for thirty years. I've even come up with a means of identifying those individuals with the greatest chance for success. Hopefully, as living empirical Life Force science proliferates, activating the Kundalini-Life Force will become an everyday occurrence.

Our race needs to make the next incremental leap in consciousness. The last leap occurred when primitive beings recognized that objects could be used as tools. Kundalini will lead us to the next incremental jump in consciousness, but a safe method must be found. At the time I met Gopi Krishna, I regret that GFM was not fully formed in my mind. Although I had practiced its techniques, I didn't have the presence of mind to connect all the dots. I didn't realize that the techniques I'd used could be shaped into a viable method. Had I realized it at the time, I'm confident Gopi Krishna would have seen its potential and that GFM would today be recognized as a safe method for permanently awakening Kundalini. The time for pioneering is over; it's time to get on with it.

So who's out there?

> I sacrifice myself and serve man, because I have presented fully this picture so that every layman and man of the world can reach it and so bring it to completion. 52

Notes

1 *Kundalini: The Evolutionary Energy in Man* – Gopi Krishna, Shambala, 1971, p. 56.

2 In this book I use Life Force and Kundalini interchangeably. Sometimes even together in the same expression: **Kundalini-Life Force**. Kundalini can be described as a great reservoir of dormant energy at the base of the spine—the creative life force. Kundalini activates the Life Force; they work together. I also use the term *Primal Spirit* as it appears in "The Secret of the Golden Flower." Every culture has a term for the Life Force entity and, although traditions may differ, the underlying principle remains the same. How could there be more than one Life Force?

3 "When Pain Remains" - Jerome Groopman - *The New Yorker*, October 10, 2005.

4 "When Pain Remains" - Jerome Groopman - *The New Yorker*, October 10, 2005.

5 "When Pain Remains" - Jerome Groopman - *The New Yorker*, October 10, 2005.

6 *The Awakening of Kundalini* – Gopi Krishna, D. B. Taraporevala Sons & Company Private Ltd., Bombay, India, 1976, p. 117.

7 Jackets without collars—worn by boys in the 1940s.

8 An X-ray machine that combines an X-ray source and a fluorescent screen to enable direct observation. Ignorance of the harmful effects of X rays resulted in the absence of standard radiation safety procedures which are employed today. Scientists and physicians would often place their hands directly in the X-ray beam resulting in radiation burns.

9 *The Secret of the Golden Flower* - Routledge & Kegan Paul, Wilhelm Translation, London, 1931, pp. 28–29.

10 "The appetite is stimulated by eating."—Rabelais.

11 Pressure Cooker.

12 *The Life of Milarepa* - Lobsang P. Lhalungpa, Shambhala, 1985, p. 41.

13 *The Secret of the Golden Flower* - Routledge & Kegan Paul, Wilhelm Translation, London, 1931, p. 29.

14 Ibid, p. 34.

15 Ibid, p. 35.

16 Ibid, p. 46.

17 Ibid, p. 52.

18 Ibid, p. 21.

19 *Kundalini: The Evolutionary Energy in Man* – Gopi Krishna, Shambala, 1971, p. 48.

20 *The Secret of the Golden Flower* - Routledge & Kegan Paul, Wilhelm Translation, London, 1931, pp. 60–61.

21 *Kundalini: The Evolutionary Energy in Man* – Gopi Krishna, Shambala, 1971, p. 57.

22 *The Secret of the Golden Flower* - Routledge & Kegan Paul, Wilhelm Translation, London, 1931, p. 22.

23 "The Book of Consciousness and Life" *The Secret of the Golden Flower* - Routledge & Kegan Paul, Wilhelm Translation, London, 1931, p. 76.

24 *The Secret of the Golden Flower* - Routledge & Kegan Paul, Wilhelm Translation, London, 1931, p. 34.

25 *The Secrets of Chinese Meditation* - Lu Kuan Yü (Charles Luk), Rider & Company, 1964, p. 194.

26 *Kundalini: The Evolutionary Energy in Man* – Gopi Krishna, Shambala, 1971, p. 53.

27 *The Biological Basis of Religion and Genius* – Gopi Krishna, Harper & Row, 1971, p. 92.

28 *Kundalini: The Evolutionary Energy in Man* – Gopi Krishna, Shambala, 1971, p. 52.

29 Ibid, p. 67.

30 *The Secret of the Golden Flower* - Routledge & Kegan Paul, Wilhelm Translation, London, 1931, p. 51.

31 *Kundalini: The Evolutionary Energy in Man* – Gopi Krishna, Shambala, 1971, p. 67.

32 Ibid, p. 74.

33 Water taxis.

34 *The Awakening of Kundalini* – Gopi Krishna, D. B. Taraporevala Sons & Company Private Ltd., Bombay, India, 1976, p. 81.

35 *Kundalini: The Evolutionary Energy in Man* – Gopi Krishna, Shambala, 1971, p. 116.

[36] My personal development work.

[37] French: A training course or internship.

[38] *12 Steps to Raw Food* - Victoria Boutenko, Raw Family Publishing, p. 63.

[39] http://www.drlockie.com/ Dr. Andrew Lockie, 1998.

[40] Induced in a patient by a physician's activity, manner, or therapy. Used especially of an infection or other complication during treatment.

[41] "Death by Medicine" - December 2003, by Gary Null, PhD, Carolyn Dean, MD ND, Martin Feldman, MD, Debora Rasio, MD, Dorothy Smith, PhD.

[42] "Is Bigger Better?" - Alice Fishburn, Newsweek, Inc., 2005.

[43] "Is Bigger Better?" - Alice Fishburn, Newsweek, Inc., 2005.

[44] Karl S. Kruszelnicki Pty Ltd 2003.

[45] In 1939, Semyon Kirlian discovered by accident that if an object on a photographic plate is subjected to a high-voltage electric field, an image is created on the plate. The image looks like a colored halo or coronal discharge. This image is said to be a physical manifestation of the spiritual aura or "life force," which allegedly surrounds each living thing.

Allegedly, this special method of "photographing" objects is a gateway to the paranormal world of auras. *The Skeptic's Dictionary*—Robert Todd Carroll.

[46] Adrian Bruce—www.adrianbruce.com

[47] Extracting Prana from air is one of the goals of Kundalini. While oxygen is available to everyone, Kundalini must be activated to extract Prana.

[48] *The Alchemy of Desire* - Tarun J. Tejpal, Picador, 2005, p. 193.

[49] "Mainstream Buddhism and Cognitive Scientists have also embarked on a long-standing investigation of the brain and the mind" Shambhala Sun, September 2005.

[50] *The Awakening of Kundalini* – Gopi Krishna, D. B. Taraporevala Sons & Company Private Ltd., Bombay, India, 1976, p. 118.

[51] "Kundalini Awareness: A Call for Scientific Research" Institute for Consciousness Research, 2005, p. 13.

[52] "The Book of Consciousness and Life" *The Secret of the Golden Flower* - Routledge & Kegan Paul, Wilhelm Translation, London, 1931, p. 73.